AF265215

A CALL TO RESTORE HIS AUTHENTIC NAME:

YAHWEH:
הוהי

Siyani Joyce Marima Shihundla

First Edition, 2020
ISBN: **978-0-620-89911-6**

Cover design and typesetting by Janet von Kleist
jvonkleist@yahoo.com

Fothane Books
fothanebooks@outlook.com
www.fothanebooks.wordpress.com

Author's contact details
Cell: +27 82 334 4271/ + 27 76 060 2954
Email: siyanima@gmail.com
Facebook account: Siyani Joyce Marima

CONTENTS

ACKNOWLEDGEMENTS

First and foremost, I submit my thanks to the Author and the Finisher of my faith — Yahweh, who inspired me to write His book. "Yahweh, who am I that You are mindful of me, the son of man that You visit me? You have crowned me with your glory and honour".

This book could not have been written without the encouragement and the help of several individuals who in one way or another contributed and extended their valuable support. My utmost gratitude goes to my spiritual coach, Prophet Jeff Khumalo whom Yahweh used to rebuke me for tarrying to carry out this assignment.

I would further like to acknowledge my friends and prayer partners who saw the potential in writing this book when I shared my dream with them: Deliwe Nyathikazi, Mumsy Mushoma and Stella Mahasha. To my fellow brother in the Lord, Rodgers Shiluvana, thank you for your encouragement.

I appreciate how my nephew, Mavona-vona, was constantly supportive and helpful in the process of writing this book. He really challenged me not to tarry. Special thanks go to my husband, Phillip Shihundla for understanding the demands of this work. My gratitude is extended to my uncle, Simon Vukela for his wisdom and constructive criticism and my cousin Maureen Baloyi for cheering me up.

I appreciate Professor Neil Snyder, who encouraged me to take the challenge, though we only talked on the phone. It will be an abomination if I do not acknowledge men of God who laid hands on me and prophesied greatness in my life: Pastor Patricia Mokoto, who departed to be with the Lord, Apostle Shiko Apwam, Pastor Johannes Motau, Reverend Jean Borsberry and Prophet Simon Mafa.

Last and not least, I would like to thank Professor Thomas Mabasa for his guidance.

EDITOR'S NOTE

The name of a being is as important as the being himself or herself. Human beings have names for a particular purpose. Your name and personal identify are intricately intertwined in such a manner that one cannot exist without the other. Your name identifies you and sets you apart from other fellow human beings. Thus, your name is not a mere collection and conjunction of letters and/or alphabets. To some extent, your name may possess the power to foretell your future and dictate your daily interaction with life and people around you. The book you are about to read reminds us about the importance of the Name of God. This book is instructive in that it educates us about the name Yahweh. It further seeks to restore our consciousness of the name ... hoping that upon learning, the reader shall use the name in prayer and other devotional activities.

In the midst of this epoch in which the names of the servants of God have somewhat subsumed the name of God, it is imperative more than ever before to re-socialise our relationship with His name — Yahweh. In this book, Siyani helps us understand that the name God is the same as in our case. Thus, using the name God is similar to being addressed as human being instead of your name. Evidently, it is erroneous to address Yahweh as God owing to the fact that God is not His name. Who would want to be addressed as human being when they have a name? None, I guess. is a go-to book for the purpose of learning about the Name Yahweh. Siyani unpacks the Names of Yahweh with the greatest simplicity there is.

An attitude of learning is critical as you are about to embark on reading this book. An open-minded stance will help you absorb and internalise practical lessons that Siyani shares in the book. It has been a blessing being part of the production of the book. I trust that you shall find it practically valuable on your journey of becoming more like Him. The scripture below will make more sense to you as you read the book.

Exodus 3: 13-14 (NIV)

Be blessed!

Ditupa Fothane

Fothane Books

www.fothanebooks.wordpress.com

FOREWORD

This book is intended to restore the genuine Name of God in the whole universe and to affirm the reader's confidence in the capacity concealed in the Name of God. It explains some of the reasons the undisputed Name of God has been hidden away from His children.

I vividly remember the first day I propped myself up against a continental pillow and felt like time stood still as I devoured each word, convinced that by some divine intersection of fate, Siyani Joyce Marima was speaking directly to me. is the second significant book on earth following the Bible that is worth reading daily.

I was excited to apply the concepts and practice referring to my Heavenly Father as Yahweh (His real Name), and as I did, a whole new world of possibilities opened up to me. I began to see visions and words that I have never seen before, or read before, neither used before when conversing and when I look them up in the dictionary I would find their meaning.

Those were not mere words, they were words relevant to the visions I had and the divine messages that rebuked me with love, guiding and ordering my footsteps. Being one of the first persons to read this book offered me an opportunity to tap into the anointing that Yahweh had discharged onto Siyani Joyce Marima. A Call to Restore His Authentic Name: Yahweh became my guide and my go-to source for inspiration, divine meditation, and empowerment. It helped me embrace spiritual inheritance I had not known I had permission to partake in.

As I read this revelation, I was struck by how some servants of the Most High God fear men to a point that they forbid other children of God from pronouncing the name Yahweh. In Proverbs 29:25 we are advised that "The fear of man is a snare, but whoever put his trust in God shall be safe".

Siyani Joyce Marima is an uncomplicated, humble and spiritually devoted daughter of The Most High God. She is a woman of courage who has a wonderful disposition. Siyani shares her journey to where she is in her spiritual evolvement through this wonderful revelation. I have been blessed in my life with many great spiritual teachers; Siyani is one of them. She is distinguishable on the basis that she can speak with and be with because of her enormous capacity to listen and offer guidance guided by the word of God, and to be in an unconditional love while rebuking with love. Siyani's spiritual teachings are from her spiritual encounters with The Most High God and she lives what she teaches.

I am deeply honoured to invite you to make this book a part of your life.

Lebogang Phildah Acedede-Selahla
Clinical Psychologist, Servant of Yahweh.
South Africa, Limpopo Province, Polokwane.

PREFACE

The book you are about to read is a call to restore the authentic Name of God, Yahweh. The Name Yahweh is a very clear description of His character as God of the covenant. The significance of His Name applies to all Christians. Yahweh is His eternal holy name that reveals His divinity. It is His unique Name. It is applied exclusively to Him. It is Yahweh's desire for His children to know His Name and the revelation it contains. The power of the Name lies in understanding the prophetic letters 'YHWH'. The mystery in the Name is hidden in the Hebrew alphabets that spell it. I am not claiming to be an expert in who Yahweh is. However, I learnt that Yahweh desires obedience more than sacrifice.

This book consists of seven chapters. The introductory chapter outlines the battle that I went through in writing this book. I really felt unfit to be an author of this topic. My resistance was short-lived hence, you are reading this book. Chapter two explains my quest to know Yahweh. His answer to my questions about who He is, birthed this book. As a new believer I was introduced to many titles of Abba Father and I wondered if

He had no name that embraces all His titles. I enquired from Him and He revealed His name. He answered me in a way I least expected, a command to write this book. Chapter three discusses religious practices and myths for concealing Yahweh's Name. In this section it suffices to know that the removal of the Name Yahweh in most Bibles is intentional. The doctrines still prevail today, however, Yahweh wants us to know and use His authentic Name.

Chapter four emphasises on the power behind the Name "Yahweh". In chapter four you will learn about how Yahweh tied His covenants, His statutes and His salvation to His Name; Yahweh further reveals His nature in His Name. Chapter five is dedicated to His nature. Chapter six discusses some of His attributes.

This book concludes by presenting Yeshua Ha Mashiach as Yahweh. The name Yeshua is the integral part of the Name Yahweh. Yeshua and Abba Father are one. He is in the Father and the Father is in Him. In addition, the statements as stated by Yeshua are discussed.

Yahweh wants His distinctive Name to be remembered forever. The purpose of this book is to restore the authentic Name of the God of the universe, Yahweh. It is meant to open the eyes of our understanding.

ONE

MY BATTLEFIELD

I had a dream on one occasion, in that dream I was given a scroll to read, unfortunately, I was unable to read what was written in the scroll. My response was that I could not read what was written. All of a sudden the letters were magnified but still, I could not read what I saw. This dream persisted for almost the first three weeks of March 2017. On the last day of the dream I recognized some of the letters in the scroll. The words I could read were YHWH and Snyder. The last part of the scroll had a clear message: "I want you to write a book about My Name "Yahweh". I woke up and recorded the dream. In my quest for more knowledge I searched the internet for YHWH and Snyder. I found that Snyder was the author of the book "His Name is Yahweh". I made a call to Dr. Snyder and shared my dream with him. He encouraged me to download the book from his web page. At that time, I was learning more about the names of God but had yet to discover the real Name and power behind the Name of God, YHWH (הוהי)

When the urge to write this book sprouted, I had started writing another book. I had to put the first one on pause in order to concentrate on this one. In my search for insight on the name YHWH, I decided to enroll for Biblical Hebrew studies. I had the zeal to know the language; I was propelled by my conviction that the scroll that I could not read had significant information. I hoped that one day when I would be able to read the language, the dream would come back and I would be able to comprehend the message. Little did I know that the phrase "YHWH" would be ammunition or a motivation enough for me to write this book. In the process of writing this book, it came to my attention that some individuals would accuse me of thinking of myself as being better than everyone else. Questions like: "Who do you think you are, writing about God's name?" would hound me on a frequent basis, reminding me of my identity in Christ.

The completion of this project was quite strenuous. I am convinced that in every good project there are characters like Sanballat and Tobiah, who would do all in their means to see the project aborted. Even in the writing of this book, I had my Sanballats and Tobiahs. All their attempts to discourage me from writing this book came to nothing. The Hebrew class that I thought would empower me about the Name Yahweh became my worse Sanballat and Tobiah.

After a year in the Biblical Hebrew class, there was no mention of the name YAHWEH. Instead, the Almighty God was referred to as Adonai (ינודא) or Elohim

(מיהולא). I got more confused when the name Adonai did not contain any of the letters that are supposed to spell the name, instead it was spelled as (הוהי) instead of ינודא. I tried to ask my teachers and his response was that it is the way it is supposed to be. Every time it was my turn to read the text in the class, I would struggle to read (הוהי) as Adonai, because my eyes and my brain did not see Adonai in the word (הוהי). I eventually had to comply. I was not satisfied with the answer and I waited for the opportune time to ask.

It happened that one day I was the only student attending the class and my teacher wanted to find out why I was interested in learning the language. I told him about my dream and the scroll. Innocently, I mentioned my yearning to know more about Yahweh. He responded by saying that I was not allowed to pronounce the Name and that I must be content with calling Him Adonai. He further warned me not to bring the topic up in the class again. The expression on his face told me that he meant it. I responded to my teacher, explaining how I was called to restore the name YAHWEH. Yahuwah knows very well who I am and He chose to reveal His Name to me. I would not know that He is Yahuwah had He not told me so. He responded, "OK, just do me a favour; do not bring this topic up in class". He further advised me to rather say Yahuwah rather than Yahweh and if possible, avoid it entirely.

I honoured my teacher's request by not bringing up the topic to class. However, I persisted and found out why the Name Yahuwah was forbidden. I had to choose whether to fear prosecution from men or to obey Yahweh who is the author and the finisher of my faith.

I made a choice to contribute to the restoration of the Name Yahweh. My decision was based on Proverbs 1: 7 which indicates that "The fear of Yahweh is the beginning of all wisdom". The Bible is also full of scriptures that emphasise that we should honour Yahweh rather than men. In Colossians 2:23 we learn that whatever we do, we must do it heartily as for Yahweh and not for men, while Acts 2:39 indicates that we ought to obey Yahweh rather than men. Proverbs 29:25 states that the fear of men brings snare, but he who put his trust in Yahweh shall be safe.

After a year I moved to another class. We were a class of two students. Our tutor, who was a Professor and a Rabbi, he was very friendly to us. Once again, it happened that I was the only student in class. I took advantage of the situation. I asked the professor about the Name Yahweh. He gave a brief lesson on the forbidden and unspeakable Name; he mentioned that he also could not say the Name. He politely told me not to mention the Name, let alone write a book about it. I noticed as he was responding to my question that he never mentioned the Name Yahweh, instead, he said Ha Shem (which means the name in Hebrew). Usually, lessons are recorded for students to be able to review, but that particular lesson was never recorded. The best that I gained from my conversation with the Professor was that the Name, (יהוה) is actually "Yahweh". Although it is spelled as Yahweh, it is pronounced as Adonai as Yahweh is considered unspeakable.

I do not regret studying Biblical Hebrew, it exposed me to the understanding of how much the name Yahweh is forbidden and considered unspeakable. Not only that, there are many mysteries in the Bible that can only be understood by the comprehension of Hebrew. The power of His name lies in speaking it. As I learnt about the Name, I learnt that historically, people who spoke the Name received the death sentence. That gave me a fright. I had mixed emotions: excitement and fear. My fears were based on the responses of Biblical Hebrew teachers. The excitement came from writing a special book and it was overwhelming. Thanks to Yahweh, my excitement overshadowed my fears and I found courage in a number of scriptures such as 2 Corinthians 10:17, it says: "But let him who glories glory in this, that He has understanding and knows Me, that I am Yahweh who exercises loving kindness, justice and righteousness in the earth, for I delight in these things, says Yahweh".

Yahweh spoke so many times through His sons and daughters about me writing this book. Some were motivational and some strongly rebuked me for tarrying on His assignment. I can testify about His patience towards me. I felt unworthy to write this book and that I was treading on dangerous territory. While contemplating whether to write the book or not, a colleague, Ms Elizabeth Mashao and her pastor friends, Emeldah Mthembi and Bridgette Falleyn visited me. One thing I enjoy doing with my visitors is to pray, after all, what I declared to Yahweh was that my house shall be a prayer house for all nations. After chatting for a while, I invited them to pray. I was praying and could not help but hear their prayers. They thanked God for choosing to reveal His name through me and when they were about to leave they simultaneously told me that they could not wait to read the book, they also mentioned how God gave me the gift of writing books. They reminded me of how I was not unworthy as I thought and that I am a vessel of honour in His eyes.

A year after, Ms Mashao's visit to my house, I still had not written a single paragraph on this book. I then visited my uncle, whom is also my advisor and told him about how I was about to write a book about the Name of God — Yahweh. He smiled at me and said, "This is your bull, you must tackle it by its horns". He gave me a month to go and write whatever the Lord would lay in my heart concerning His name. On the set date I had an outline of what to write about and honoured the appointment I had with my uncle. I brought the manuscript with me however; he did not even look at it. He just said, "your bull is too thin, go and fatten it, then we can talk about how to avoid its horns from goring you". I thank Yahweh for his wisdom. Today I have a bull with trimmed horns.

Writing this book was highly fulfilling to me. In December 2019, I attended a church conference where my fear of publishing this book was uttered through Prophet Elijah Mathebula. Prophet Elijah prophesied and said: "I see you learning an ancient language; this language is written from right to left. I see you writing a book, yes, the book is finished. I see the Name Yahweh on the book. I see another book that you have started, it is linked to the name Yahweh, I see another one, and this is about your personal testimony. Go on and do what God has assigned you to do". I could relate to all that He told me.

I regularly watch The Sid Roth television show; he states: "God is provoking Jews to jealousy", paraphrasing Romans 10:19-20, which reads, "I will move them to jealousy with those who are not a people, I will provoke them to anger with a foolish nation" (19). And Isaiah is very bold and says, I am found by those who didn't seek Me. I said, see me, see me to a nation that was not called by my Name" (20).

Sid Roth's statement gives me a deeper revelation of Yahweh's intention with this book. Yahweh wants all of His sons to have a personal relationship with Him. If I, Siyani Joyce Marima, from a rural village, Eka Hasani Dakari, which even my fellow South Africans are unfamiliar with, have been granted the privilege to restore His Name, what more about the Jewish people who were supposed to give us light about His Name?

Let this be the jealousy that will cause many people to willingly have a personal relationship with Yeshua. It is through Yeshua that we gain permission to call the name Yahweh, let this be the jealousy that will make us run back to the loving arms of Abba Father.

This book is meant to replace the names LORD, GOD or Adonai with His real Name Yahweh or Yahuwah. In this book the Names Yahuwah and Yahweh will be used interchangeably for they hold the same meaning. You may choose to call Him LORD or GOD; at least you are informed.

Considering that I rather fear Yahweh over being threatened by my teacher, I chose to honour and please Yahweh rather than my teacher. I pondered on a scripture in John 9:4 that reads: "I must work the works of Him who created me while it is day; the night is coming when no one can work".

It took me a while to make the decision. Thanks to Yahweh who sent some of His prophets to speak to me about my unfinished business - a book that I was delaying to write. My spiritual mentor, Jefferson Khumalo, spoke so strong about this and said, "Do you think you are very special to God? If you refuse to write the book, God will choose someone else to write exactly what He told you to write. God is not short of authors but He wants you to be the one to deliver His message". The words were spoken to me at the time that I had ceased writing the book. Yahweh used three prophets who rebuked me for disobedience. The strongest words were: "Stop praying to God and say use me if you're not prepared to take His instruction".

Thanks to my Pastor, Prophet Jeff Khumalo who gave me a wake-up call. One day he called me and said, "Believe in your God, and you shall be established, believe in His prophets, and you shall prosper. If you do not do what God has told you, He will find someone else to do it. Why have you stopped writing His book? Do not tarry".

I had to repent and ask for courage. Then I re-membered the scripture that says, "Yahweh chose the foolish things of the world to put to shame the wise; Yahweh has chosen the weak things of the world to put to shame the mighty and the base things of the world and the things that I despised Yahweh has cho-sen, and that things that are not, to bring nothing the things are, that no flesh should glory in His Presence" (1 Corinthians 1:27-29).

Furthermore, His word in John 15:5-11 echoed in my spirit: "I am the vine, you are the branches; he who abides in Me and I in him, he bears much fruit, for apart from Me you can do nothing. If anyone does not abide in Me, he is thrown away as a branch and dries up; and they gather them, and cast them into the fire and they are burned. If you abide in Me, and My words abide in you, ask whatever you wish, and it will be done for you. My Father is glorified by this, that you bear much fruit, and so prove to be My disciples. Just as the Father has loved Me, I have also loved you; abide in My love. If you keep My commandments, you will abide in My love; just as I have kept My Father's commandments and abide in His love. These things I have spoken to you so that My joy may be in you, and that your joy may be made full".

Had it not been for the prophets of God I could have missed the opportunity to bear fruits for Yahweh. I now take it as an opportunity to glorify Yahweh. What a privilege it is to abide in His love, to have His joy in me and I mean full joy. It might have taken too long for me to realise that I am the chosen vessel for this task; however, I am grateful I obeyed at last.

There is no way I could not continue with this book after reading the scripture that says: "But if some of the branches were broken off, and you, being a wild olive, were grafted in among them and became partaker with them of the rich root of the olive tree, do not be arrogant toward the branches; but if you are arrogant, remember that it is not you who supports the root, but the root supports you. Yahweh's thoughts are not our thoughts, nor our ways His ways, for as the heavens are higher than the earth so are His ways higher than our ways and His thoughts higher than our thoughts" (Isaiah 55:8-9).

Long before I was born, Yahweh had me in mind to write this book. He foreknew. Romans 8:28 -30 states: "We know that all things work together for good for those who are called according to His purpose (28). We also know that "For whom He foreknew, He also predestined to be conformed to the image of His Son, that He might be the firstborn among many brothers" (29). Whom He predestined, those He also called, those He also justified. Whom He justified those He also glorified."

I feel so humbled to have been chosen for this assignment. Definitely Yahweh has chosen me to make a call to restoring His Name. Indeed, I tarried but eventually the message is delivered. Glory is to Him who made me overcome all my fears and doubts of my ability to carry this assignment.

TWO

MY QUEST TO KNOW HIM

I was introduced to the (many or various) names of God within three months of receiving Him as my Lord and Saviour. The inspiration was triggered by a song I heard in church. The song was about Jehovah Nissi as bigger than what people say. When we left church that day, my sister told me that she had noticed how I was not singing when the song was sung; I told her that I had never heard of "Johannes" in the Bible, so I did not want to glorify a god that I do not know. Her explanation exposed my ignorance and that turned to be a form of motivation for me to want to know the names of God. The song was about the greatness of Jehovah Nissi and not "Johannes". The more I learnt about the many names of God, the more I thirst to know Him. I started reading the Bible in search of His names and I would highlight each name I came across.

In my quest to know God, I read many books including the Bible in search of who He is. Whenever I wanted to learn something new about Him, I would refer to Jeremiah 33:3 and pray. At the time my prayer point was "Father, your word says I should call on You, and You will answer me, and show me great and unsearchable things I do not know. Now I ask you in the name of Yeshua to show me great and mighty things that I do not know. Father I want to know your Name, reveal your Name to me." As an answer to my prayer, I would either have a vision, a dream or a scripture that would be laid in my heart and occasionally, somebody would share the word with me.

In search of who He is, I became a God-chaser. I would at least attend three services every Sunday. Sometimes, this would have been at different churches. The more I pursued Him, the hungrier and thirsty for Him I became. Should there have been a conference around Pretoria or Johannesburg and I happened to have heard about it, I would not have missed it at any cost. I pursued Him in prayer and in studying the Bible. My office became a prayer house for all nations. We would sacrifice our lunch time for prayer. Yahweh honoured the prayer meetings by enabling healing to take place and some people received the baptism of the Holy Spirit. In case you were wondering if my chasing was worth it, well, I am not finished yet. I am still chasing after Him. Every day I yearn for intimacy with Him. Not only intimacy, but the highest possible level of intimacy.

Within a year of my salvation I had read through the Bible. I responded to a call in Isaiah 55: "Hey! Come, everyone who thirsts, to the waters! Yes, come, buy wine and milk without money and without price".

Just like a deer pants for water brooks, my soul panted for God. My soul was thirsty for the living God. I proclaimed Psalm 63:1 saying: "God, you are my God, I will earnestly seek You. My soul thirsts for you. My flesh longs for. You in a dry and weary land where there is no water." My quest was driven by the desire to have a personal relationship with God. In spite of what Yahweh was doing in our midst, I realised how much more I needed to know Him.

The next question that I asked Yahweh was, "God I know that you have so many names. Do you not have one that embraces all your names?" In response to my question, I had a series of dreams for about three weeks. This dream was about a scroll that would be placed before me. The content of the scroll was in a language that I could not read. I would always state how I could not read what was written on the scroll. I would notice a foreign letter being magnified; however, I still could not read what was on the scroll. The last time I had been specific in my response I said that I did see what was written, however I could not read the language. Almost immediately, some letters changed to "YHWH" and the word Snyder appeared. This section has been narrated in the last chapter. It is repeated as an acknowledgement of the birth of this book.

Yahweh's thoughts are not our thoughts nor are our ways His ways. As the heavens are higher than the earth, so are His ways. He answered my prayers, yet I did not perceive it. I did not expect His answer to be in an unknown language, Hebrew. What I extracted from this book is that all the other names that we historically called Him were and still are His titles and mainly, describe what He is capable of doing. Simply put, they are describing His roles and characters (Snyder, 2011). Some of His titles are attached as "Annexure". Whatever His role or character may be, He does not have any limit. He is who He is and does what He pleases. I had also learnt that our God has a real name. His Name is Yahuwah/Yahweh. In my ignorance, I knew the Name of God as Yahweh and that Yahweh is Jehovah. However, I did not know the profound power it carries.

I feel so humbled to inform you that God of the universe has a Name. God is not His name; it is His nature. His Name is Yahuwah/ Yahweh, (YHWH: יהוה). To put it in simple terms, you are a human being; however, "human-being" is not your name. Human being is your nature but you have a name that distinguishes you from other people. The name of God as we call Him is His being. It is the equivalent of you as a human being. That is correct.

After going through the book by Snyder (2011) and learning that "Yahweh" was replaced by the words LORD or GOD, it became clear that the divine Name of Yahweh was known before Moses and the burning bush. Genesis 2:4 sums up the history of the creation of heaven and earth and also acknowledged Yahweh as their creator. In Genesis 4:26 we are also told that after the birth of Enosh, men began to call on the name of the LORD, that is, Yahweh. Further, in Genesis 13:4. Abram built an altar and called on the name of the LORD. Isaac also built an altar and called on the name of the LORD (Genesis 26:25). Now that you know that the name

LORD is a substitute for Yahweh, you will agree with me that the patriarchs called the Name Yahweh.

When Yahweh appeared to Moses, He introduced Himself as the God of his fathers, the God of Abraham, the God of Isaac and the God of Jacob. It is clear that Moses' fathers, namely, Abraham. Isaac and Jacob knew the real name of God. The revelation that I got from this was that at that time, Yahweh's name was no longer in use. He was rather known as God of Abraham, Isaac and Jacob. It was for this reason that Moses said to Yahweh, "Indeed when I come to the children of Israel and say to them the God of your fathers has sent me to you and they say to me: What is His name, what shall I say to them?" Yahweh's response to Moses was, "I AM WHO I AM. Thus you shall say I AM has sent me to you" (Exodus 3:13:14).

Yahweh is a Hebrew name meaning, I AM THAT I AM. YAHWEH is identified as God's personal Name, or His Divine Name. YAHWEH is called the Tetragrammaton, a four-letter word, because it has four letters in Hebrew. His Name YAHWEH sets Him apart by distinguishing between Him and anything or anyone else. Yahweh's Name, "I AM that I AM", reveals the fullness of His nature. All of Yahweh's nature and attributes are embodied in His Name. Not only did I gain a wealth of knowledge from Snyder (2011) but I was motivated to learn more about the name. In my quest to know His name I enrolled for Biblical Hebrew lessons.

This might seem to be like air to a bird. You may be wondering what the big deal is. I hope to be able to show you just how big a deal it is, and what it means for you and me. The Name Yahweh denotes His creative power over the cosmos. Yahweh exists and echoes in all dimensions of life. He exists in the human being, human body, life, the world and in the cosmos.

Yahweh is the name that has been forbidden and removed from the Bible. I believe that their actions are aligned to the scripture in 2 Timothy 4:3-4: "For the time will come when people will not put sound doctrine. Instead to suit their own desires they will gather around them a number of teachers to say what their itching ears want to hear. So they will turn their ears away from the truth and turn aside to myths".

The Jews would not say Yahweh. Instead, they would say HASHEM which is a Hebrew word that means "The Name". Yahweh is also called the ineffable or the unspeakable Name. Yahweh is not unspeakable. The Name carries power that is beyond human comprehension. In fact, according to the Bible, Yahweh commanded us to tell the world who He is by name (Snyder, 2011). Snyder (2011) further explains that Yahweh means I WAS, I AM and I WILL BE and "I AM" is His only real Name. "I AM" is also the definition of His Name. His Name Yahweh sets Him apart by distinguishing between Him and anything or anyone else.

Yahweh (I AM THAT I AM) describes the following about God:

- He who is
- The self-existent one, and
- He who is ever becoming what He is

Yahweh has also been interpreted as He who makes that which has been made. He who brings into existence whatever exits (ancient.eu/Yahweh). When we mention His name we proclaim that He exists forever in every moment and He will exist for all eternity.

Yahweh is He who existed before all things. He is existence and self-existent. He was not created but always existed, He is the creator. He exists and echoes in all dimensions of life. He exists in the universe and gives life to all its occupants, "For by Him were all things created, that are in heaven, that are in earth visible and invisible, whether they be thrones, or dominion, or principalities, or powers, all were created by Him and for Him" (Colossians 1:16-17). As reflected in human beings, the source of all creation has no beginning or end. He is whoever and forever becoming what He is.

What the Name says about Him is that He will be what He is meant to be. His Name is an invitation for us fellowship with Him. The Name is a promise that we will get to know Him along the way. It talks about His desire for us to have personal experience of Him. His Name says "You have to experience Me and get to know Me as you walk in Me".

Yahweh is the source of all being and is inherent in Himself. Yahweh is beyond all predications or attributes of language; He is the source of all possible utterance. He is beyond all descriptions. His being and His name are inseparable. His name Yahweh declares that He is called by His actions. Yahweh exists in human beings, in the cosmos in the letters "YHWH".

In ancient Hebrew, letters were written in pictographs. The first letter in the name YHWH is called Yod. The pictograph writing of a Yod looks like a closed hand. Yod is the smallest letter in the Hebrew alphabet. It is similar to an apostrophe hanging on air ('). Though the Yod is the smallest letter, it consists of three parts. The head representing Yahweh, the middle part holds the parts together, symbolising unity and the lower part points towards the earth, His creation. Yod is considered a starting point of Yahweh in all things. Yod is contained in every letter. It also indicates Yahweh's omnipresence (Hebrew4chistians.com).

The second letter H is called (Hey). It is the fifth letter of the alphabets. Hey (h) is written as follows :(ה). The pictograph of the letter H looks like a man with raised arms. According to Jewish mystics, hey represents divine breath, revelation, victory and light. The word light appears five times in Genesis 1:3–5 representing its numerical value. The numerical value in our bodies represents five fingers, five senses and the five dimensions. On the spiritual level it represents five levels of our souls, namely:

- Nefesh – instincts
- Ruach – emotions
- Neshemah – mind
- Chayah – breach to transcendence
- Yechida – oneness

The letter Hey also represents the following:

- Yahweh's creative power
- The breath of His mouth (Psalm 33:6)
- The picture of God within the human heart
- The picture of the Spirit of God indwelling in the believer, (https://www.hebrew4christians.com/Grammar/)

The third letter in YHWH is "W" pronounced as vav; it is written as follows, (ו). Vav is the sixth letter in the Hebrew alphabet. The pictograph of Vav looks like a tent page or a nail. The letter Vav appears in Genesis 1:1. The placement of Vav in Genesis1:1 denotes its essential connective powers. It connects heaven and earth. It entails to the connection and earthly matters. The Vav is the connecting force or the divine hook that binds together heaven and earth.

The last letter is H. The repetition of the word H emphasises all that is described in the first letter H.

Yahweh is reflected in the human body as the letters represent the human structure. The Yod is the head, this is the letter that also defines Yahweh's infinity; the 1st Hey (h) is the arm, the waw or vav is the torso, the second Hey (h) is the legs (lower limbs). In life, the Yod is the intellect, the first Hey (h) is the desire and the vav is the animation. The second Hey is the emotions (hebrew4christians.com/Grammar Unit).

In the cosmos, His name represents the orderly and harmonious wholeness of the world. His name embraces all that He created in Genesis 1. That whistle, the awe that one makes when we admire the beauty of nature, reflects His Name.

THREE

RELIGIOUS PRACTICES AND MYTHS FOR CONCEALING YAHWEH'S NAME

The next question I asked myself was, if God's name is Yahuwah, how come His name does not appear in the Bibles I read? This is a seriously hidden secret to most of us Christians. Yahuwah says, "He who made the earth and He who formed and established it, Yahweh is His Name Call to me and I will answer you and tell you great and unsearchable things you do not know" (Jer.33:2-3). Yahweh's word in Deut. 29:29 further says: "The secret things belong to Yahweh our God but the things revealed belong to us and our children forever".

Ryrie in Snyder (2011) states that Yahweh's Name appears in Hebrew manuscripts of Old Testament exactly 6 823 times. However, the Name is concealed in the scriptures. The Name "Yahweh" does not even appear once in most Bibles such as: the King James,

New International Version or the Amplified. In these Bibles, the Name Yahweh should appear where the word "LORD or GOD" appears.

Snyder (2011) alludes that Yahweh's Name was used extensively in Israel until the mid-second century B.C. According to literature, Yahweh, as the authentic Name of the supreme being, seems to have remained in use until the Babylonian exile and the destruction of the temple(Reb jeff.com,). There was a time when the Name Yahweh was pronounced by all of Yahweh's people, in prayers, in blessings, and in greetings. However, by the third century B.C.E., our teachers began teaching that Yahweh, the true Name of our Creator, was too holy to pronounce. [1]This teaching is a practice that was not inspired by our Father, but one that gradually came about due to pagan influence.

In an attempt to find out why the use of Yahweh's Name has been abolished, I found from sources that the Jews have been taught not to use the Name for various reasons. Some of the reasons include the following:
- The Name considered unpronounceable
- The rabbis after 70 C.E introduced the injunction "Thou shall not use the Name of Yahweh".
- The Name contained fearsome power and that its misuse could bring destruction on its speaker and others.

A systematic decision was then made that the Name be no longer spoken. As a result, the Name of Yahweh has almost been forgotten (in effect, profaned or brought to nothing (masacc.edu/divine-name, html).

---

1. www.yahweh.com

It is recorded that the pronunciation of the Name Yahweh began to be suppressed upon the death of a man named Simeon the Just, a High Priest who served in the time span of 310–199 B.C.E., or about 200 years before the nation of Israel came under the rulership of the Roman Empire. The Jewish Encyclopaedia (1901) points out that this was the turning point, namely the exact time when it became a practice in Israel to no longer pronounce the Name Yahweh (www.yahweh. com).

It is alleged that the Israelites are taught not to pronounce the Holy Name of our Creator and Father, Yahweh. Yet, it is the Name that Yahweh chooses to be known by. Yahweh is the most powerful Name. He intended to be called by it. This is the Name that brings deliverance for those who call upon Him. The Israelites are instructed by their teachers that Yahweh's name is too holy to pronounce; therefore, they call Him "Adonai" or "Elohim". The teaching has been fully ingrained in the minds of nearly all Israelites to the point that extreme hatred is shown toward anyone who openly speaks or writes about the one and only true Name of the Creator. Important to note is that the holy prophets in the Bible spoke and wrote about the true Name. They proclaimed the messages in the Yahweh's Name.

It was not until I started searching for the reason why the Name Yahweh was forbidden that I realised the sensitivity of the topic. I realised that I am entering into a dangerous territory, at some point I wanted to stop writing this book. I felt so irrelevant handling this topic. I strongly felt that this topic should be addressed by people of apostle Paul's calibre who identified himself circumcised on the eighth day, of the nation of Israel, of the tribe of Benjamin, a Hebrew of Hebrews; as to the Law, a Pharisee (Phil 3: 5). I wondered if indeed I heard from Yahweh that I should write this book. I went to my journal where I had recorded my conversation with Yahweh about writing this book. There it was, I had scribbled the picture that I saw in my dream. My argument was that Snyder (2011) has already written the book "His name is Yahweh", why should I duplicate? Of course, it is more on emphasising the point and the text is not exactly the same.

This is a seriously hidden secret to most of us as Christians. Yahweh is the creator and Redeemer. "Yahweh your Redeemer, and He who formed you from the womb says, I am Yahweh who makes all things, who alone stretches the heavens, who spreads out the earth by Myself" (Isaiah 44:24). Yahweh says, "Look to Me, and be saved, all ends of the earth, for I am God, and there is no other" (Isaiah 45:22). Prohibiting the use of the Name is based on myths. The fallacies for prohibiting the use of the name Yahweh is well captured in Snyder (2011) and they are as follows:

- It is too sacred
- We are not required to use it
- It has no value
- Yahuwah/Yahweh is a Hebrew Name, and people who did not speak Hebrew are not required to use it
- What will make them to be able to say "Yahweh"
- Only Jews are required to use the Name Yahweh

- Yeshua and His disciples did not use the Name Yahweh. Jehovah is the Name of God mostly commonly used today God knows when we are addressing Him, so the name we use is unimportant
- God had not convicted me personally about the importance of using the Name Yahweh
- Moses was the first person to use the Name Yahweh, so the Name itself is not eternal.

Yahweh has empowered me to bring back His Name. Based on the Jewish Tradition of forbidding the Name, the argument does not hold water. They are just fallacies. I think it is an act of chasing after wind. What matters is that Yahweh wants His Name back fulltime. The fallacies are counter-acted below:

It is too sacred: The fact that the Name is too sacred does not call for its extinction. Instead, its sacredness should be the basis for honouring it. Having full knowledge of the sacredness of His Name calls us to use it with reverent worship and fear.

Exodus 20:7 tells us that we must not use the Name of Yahweh in vain, for He will not hold him guiltless who takes His Name in vain. Further in Leviticus 19:12 we are told not to swear by His Name falsely or profane it.

Yahweh never prohibited us to call His Name. The use of the Name Yahuwah is the beginning and principal and choice of knowledge paraphrased in Proverbs 1:7. Throughout the Bible, Yahweh is instructing people to use His Name. He makes a call for us to chant praises, to proclaim His Name and He speaks highly of one who knows His Name as shown in the scriptures below:

1. Psalm 68 reads: "Sing praises to Yahweh! Sing praises to His name! Extol him who rules the clouds (4). Yah His name! Rejoice before Him (5)'. Further in Psalm 95: an invitation is sent to sing to Yahweh and reads "Oh come let us sing to Yahweh. Let us shout aloud to the rock of our salvation" (1). Psalm 96 also calls us to sing to Yahweh and reads: "Sing to Yahweh a new song! Sing to Yahweh all earth (1) Sign to Yahweh! Bless His name!" (2).

2. Psalm 105 is so rigorous about us calling the Name of Yahweh. It reads: "Give thanks to Yahweh! Call on His name! (1), sing to Him, sign praises to Him. Tell of His marvellous works (2), Glory in His holy name. Let the heart of those who seek Yahweh rejoice. Seek Yahweh and His strength, Seek His face forever more".

3. Isaiah 12: "In that day you will say, give thanks to Yahweh. Call on His name. Declare His doings among the peoples. Proclaim that His name is exalted (4). Sing to Yahweh for He has done excellent things. Let this be known in all the earth" (5).

We are not required to use it. The notion that we are not required to use it is a misconception. The Name has been called since the birth of Enosh (Genesis 4:26). Yahweh wants us to call on His Name. His Name is tantamount to our salvation. In Isaiah 43:11 and 13, He says, "I myself am Yahweh. Besides me there is no saviour (11). Yes, since the day, I AM HE, there is no one who can deliver out of My hand, I will work, and who can hinder it?"

Yahweh intended His name to communicate His nature forever. When Yahweh introduced the Name to Moses in Exodus 3:15, He said: "You shall tell the children of Israel this, Yahweh the God of your fathers, the God of Abraham, the God of Isaac, and the God of Jacob, has sent me to you. This is My name forever, and this is My memorial to all generations. In Psalm 83: 18 it is written: "That they may know that you alone whose name is Yahweh are the Most High of all the earth". Emphasis is also put in Psalm 135:13: "Your name, Yahweh endures forever, your renown Yahweh throughout generations". He intended it to be remembered forever.

The Name Yahweh is the power unto our salvation. Joel 2:32 reads: "It will happen that whoever will call on Yahweh's name shall be saved, for in Mount Zion and in Jerusalem there will be those who escape, as Yahweh has said, and among the remnant, those whom Yahweh calls". The first part of the same scripture is repeated in Romans 10:13 as follows: "Whoever will call on the name of Yahweh will be saved".

Psalm 91 emphasises this point thus: "Because he has set his love on me, therefore I will deliver him. I will set him on high because he has known My name (14). He will call on me, and I will answer him, I will be with him in trouble, I will deliver him, and honour him (15). I will satisfy him with long life and show him My salvation" (16). Without any shadow of doubt knowing and calling on Yahweh's Name is the key to our salvation and deliverance.

There are a number of passages in the Bible that command us to call upon the Name of Yahweh. Some of the examples are:

- Oh give thanks to Yahweh. Call His name. Make what He has done known among the people (1 Chronicles 16: 8).
- Psalm 55:16 says, "As for me I will call on God, Yahweh will save me".

We also learn about how Jonah prayed to Yahweh his God out of the fish's belly and said: "I called because of my affliction to Yahweh, He answered me. Out of the belly of the Sheol I cried to Yahweh; you heard my voice (Jonah 2:1)".

The least you can do is know that Abba Father's real name is Yahweh. You may choose not to call Him as such, however, you are informed. A simple example is if someone asks you who is your father, referring to your biological father, you will tell them your father's real name, and not his title. His word in Ezekiel 39 reads: "So I will make my holy name known in the midst of My people, Israel, and will not make them profane My holy name anymore. Then the nations shall know that I am know that I am Yahweh, the Holy One in Israel (7). Behold, it come, and it will be done, says the Lord Yahweh. This is the day about which I have spoken" (8). If Yahweh says so, so it is so.

It has no value. Yahweh is the most powerful Name ever. This is the Name that holds His eternal essence. His Name embraces the weight of His character and significance. Yahweh (יהוה) is the Name that He revealed to us so we may know who He is. Saying that the Name has no value is blasphemy to His nature. The value of His Name is seen in that most of His compound titles. However, in most of the Bible His compound titles are replaced by Jehovah. For example, Jehovah Jireh should read Yahweh Jireh instead. If the Name does not have any value, He should not have revealed it to Moses as in Exodus 3; let alone that He chose to reveal it to me as His adopted child. Look at all the incidents in the scriptures when Yeshua proclaimed the I AM, and observe what followed after that. Yahweh is His authentic Name. It is His original and meaningful Name. It carries His essential nature.

Yahweh is the Name that He used when He made covenants with the patriarchs in the Old Testament. For example, He used His Name when He made a covenant with creation through Noah (Genesis 8:20-22). In the covenant, Yahweh declared that He will never again curse the ground for man's sake and that the seasons of the year shall not cease. In Genesis 9, Yahweh made a covenant with Noah after the flood that the waters shall never again become a flood to destroy all flesh. The rainbow that Yahweh promised as a sign of remembering His covenant still stands today. Yahweh as a covenant God made a number of covenants with Abraham. He made a covenant to multiply Abraham exceedingly (Genesis 17:1- 4). In the same chapter, Genesis 17:1, Yahweh also made a covenant of circumcision with him (Abraham). To date, the Jews still uphold the tradition of circumcision of male children on the 8th day after birth.

Yahweh is embedded in many of His titles, for example:

1. YHWH YIREH:
(GOD OUR PROVIDER)

Abraham's most significant test of faith was to take his promised son Isaac to Mount Moriah, to bind and sacrifice him as Yahweh commanded him to do. However, Yahweh brought salvation to Isaac by providing a replacement sacrifice, that is, a ram stuck in the bush. This is accounted for in Genesis 22:13-14: "Then Abraham lifted his eyes and looked , and there behind him was a ram caught in the thicket by its horns, so Abraham went and took the ram, and offered it for a burnt offering instead of his son. And Abraham called the name of the place Yahweh will provide, as it is said today. In the Mount of the Yahweh it shall be provided". This is what the title Yahweh Yireh derives from. I believe it is because of the value in the Name of Yahweh that it was removed from scripture. Yahweh is the source of life.

2. YHWH TZIDKENU
(GOD OUR RIGHTEOUSNESS)

The Jewish people from time immemorial to date celebrate the day of the atonement (Yom Kippur) as it is one of the laws in the book of Leviticus. It is stated: "On this day atonement (Yom Kippur] will be made for you, to cleanse you. Then, before the Yahweh, you will be clean from all your sins." (Leviticus 16:30). On this day the nation collectively repented to Yahweh Tzidkenu. Yom Kippur is still the most holy time of the year for the Jewish people, and it denotes a very real need for salvation in a way transcending the mere physical. I believe this practice is maintained because of the realisation of the power in the Name Yahweh Tzidkenu. Some of the compound titles of Yahweh are attached as Annexure A.

The value in the Name is also stressed in most Hebrew names. The shortened form "Yahw" occurs in many personal names in the Bible, such as Elijah (Hebrew: Eliyyahu: My God Yahu), Isaiah (Hebrew Yehsa /Yahu: salvation of Yahu). Another shortened form becomes Y'ho in names such as Joshua (Y'hoshua: Yahu is salvation) and Jehoshaphat (Y'hoshaphat: Yahu is judge). There is also an abbreviated form that includes "Ye", it begins the personal names and Yah end the name. For example, Jehu (Yehu: Yah is He) and Jesus (Yeshua: Yah is salvation). Another type of the abbreviation is "Yo" which is found in names such as Joel (Yo'el: Yahu is God) and Joram (Yoram: Yahu is exalted (Kubik, 2016). Yahweh's name is more than important. It sets Him apart by distinguishing between Him and anything or anyone else. It sets Him apart from any idol and from any other lords. Yahweh's Name is a strong tower, the righteous run to Him and they are safe.

Let me expound on some of the myths that I mentioned earlier.

> **Yahuwah/Yahweh is a Hebrew name, and people who did not speak Hebrew are not required to use it.**

Yahweh is not Yahweh of the Hebrews only, although the Hebrews prohibited the use of the Name. The Name Yahweh is highly accessible to all nations, which in turn, makes it easier to mention. The words that are in His name are adorned with the power of who He is. The power in His Name is meant to benefit all. He is Yahweh — the God of all mankind (Jeremiah 32:27). In Psalm 19:1- 4a, Yahweh says: "The heavens declare the glory of Yahweh and the firmament shows His handiwork. Day unto day utters speech and night unto night reveals knowledge. There is no speech no language where their voice is not heard, their lines have gone out throughout the earth and their words to the end of the world." Yahweh is God of the universe. Psalm 24:1 proclaims, "The earth is Yahweh's with its fullness, the world and those who dwell in it". Psalm 104:24 reads: "Yahweh, how many are your works? In wisdom you have made them all. The earth is full of your riches".

Included in His creation are all people. It is true that there are diverse languages in the world and Hebrew is one of them, so is my mother tongue, Xitsonga. That said, He assigned me to restore His Name. Restoring His Name means using the Name in prayer, in worship, and in thanksgiving. If the universe is able to call on all other titles of Yahweh, what will make them not to be able to say Yahweh? Yahweh wants all people to call His name. It is His will that His name be great among the Gentiles. Malachi 1:11 reads: "From the rising of the sun, even to its going down, y name shall be great among the Gentiles. In every place incense shall be offered to Your name and a pure offering. For My name shall be great among the nations says Yahweh of Armies".

> ## What will make them to be able to say "Yahweh?

Nobody knows for sure how to pronounce or spell the Name today. Even if the original name was known, names are often translated, pronounced, and spelt differently from one language to another. Besides, the importance is not in the pronunciation but in the meaning. Yahweh has given all of us knowledge and understanding. As His creation, He made us with a high degree of aptitude; therefore, we are all able to comprehend. We are His creation, His Spirit rests upon us. As a result, Yeshua Ha Mashiach abides in us and we are in Him. We have the Spirit of wisdom and understanding, the Spirit of counsel and might, the Spirit of knowledge and the Spirit of fear of Yahweh as reflected in Isaiah 11:2.

> ## Only Jews are required to use the Name Yahweh.

Surely Yahweh has made those who are not His people, His people. All believers are in Christ Yeshua, and He is in all of us. Yeshua is in the Father and the Father in Him. Yeshua says, "I and My Father are one" (John 10.30). Romans 11:11 says that, "Through their trespass (Hebrews) salvation has come to the Gentiles, so as to make Israel jealous". The argument that only the Jews are required to use the Name Yahweh overlooks the scripture (davar/ word) in Galatians 3: "There is neither, Jews nor Greek, neither slave nor free, nor is there male or female, for you are all one in Christ Yeshua" (28). If you are in Christ's, then you are Abraham's offspring and heirs according to the promise" (29).

Important to note is that all scripture is Yahweh breathed and profitable for reproof, for correction, and for instructions in righteousness. If Yahweh is in the scripture, the Holy Spirit who is assigned with teaching responsibility will teach all who need to call upon the Name of Yahweh how to call it. Besides, I heard a lot of people struggling to pronounce other people's names but that does not change who they are. Noticeable is that the same Jews, who are said to be required to use the Name, are the ones who have abandoned and prohibited its use.

> **Yeshua and His disciples did not use the Name Yahweh.**

It seemed to have slipped the minds of those who forbid the Name of Yahweh that Yeshua Himself is Yahweh. Yeshua particularly used the Name Yahweh. The truth is that the Name Yahweh is not recorded in most Bibles. The Name has been indeed substituted by His titles. In most Bibles the Name Yahweh is replaced by LORD or GOD. It took someone's boldness to forbid the use of the Name "Yahweh". Tradition successfully managed to forbid the use of His authentic Name. Subsequently, succeeding in causing the Jewish to pronounce His special Name) (הוהי() as Adonai. Yeshua called Yahweh Him Father acknowledging the Godhead of Yahweh. Yeshua and Yahweh are one. Yeshua is in Yahweh and Yahweh is in Him.

Considering that the name of Abba Father has been concealed, Yeshua and His disciples used the name of Abba Father. There are many passages where Yeshua quoted scriptures in the Old Testament where the name of Yahweh was used. Below are some of the examples:

Yeshua did call the Name Yahweh. As already indicated, there are some instances where He referred to the Name while quoting the Old Testament. While Yeshua was responding to a group of Pharisees who had a question on how could David call His Descendant Lord. Quoting Psalm 110:1, He said to them, "How does David in the Spirit call Him Lord (43), saying Yahweh said to My Lord, sit at My right hand, until I put My enemies beneath Your feet?" (44). In John 4a when Yeshua announced His earthly ministry, He said, "The Spirit of Yahweh is upon Me, because Yahweh He has appointed e to preach the gospel to the poor."

Further, in Mark 12:29 - 30 and Luke 10:27, Yeshua responding to the scribes in the presence of many witnesses, quoted Deuteronomy 6:4-5: "The first commandment is, Hear oh Israel, Yahweh our God is one".

In John 5:43 when Yeshua prayed for His disciples He said, " I have come in Your Father's Name and do not receive Me. If another comes in His own name you will receive". Further in His prayer in John 17, He said, "I have manifested Your Name to men whom You have given Me, and have kept your word (6). Now I am no longer in the world, but these are in the world, and I came to You. Holy Father keep them through Your Name those whom You have given Me: that they may be one as We are one (11). While I was with them, in the world, I kept Your Name. Those whom you gave

Me I have kept and none of them is lost except the son of perdition that the scripture may be fulfilled" (12). Furthermore, there is no scripture where Yeshua called the name Jehovah that is commonly used in most Bibles. Besides, it is common practice to not call fathers with their names. Fathers are called dad, daddy or papa. Yeshua often referred to Yahweh as Father and not by His Name.

My observation is that neither did Yeshua's disciples call Him by His name Yeshua (Jesus). They called Him Rabbi or Lord. Some of the scriptures where His disciples referred to Him as Rabbi include the following:

- John 1:38 details the recruitment of His first two disciples; it states that reads: "Jesus turned and saw them following, and said to them: What are you looking for? They said to Him Rabbi (which is being translated Teacher) where are you staying"?
- John 4:31, His disciples found Him after His conversation with the Samaritan woman; it reads: "In the meanwhile, the disciples urged Him, saying Rabbi eat".
- In Matthew 17:4 and Mark 9:5 when Yeshua was transfigured on the mount; we read: "Then Peter answered and said to Yeshua, Rabbi, it is good for us to be here. If you wish, let us make three tabernacles: one for You, one for Moses and one for Elijah".
- In John 21 when He asked Peter if he loved Him, Peter's response was, "Yes Lord, You know that I love You (15 and 16). The point I am driving is, why is it an issue for people to call Yahweh

by His Name? Yet it is so simple for us to call Yeshua by His Name even though His disciples called Him Rabbi or Lord.

> **Jehovah is the name of God most-ly commonly used today.**

Yes, this is true, but we call Him Jehovah because someone decided to hide or forbid His original Name to us. Abba Father's Name derives from the Hebrew letters "yod-hey- waw-hey". These four letters are known as the Tetragrammaton (Greek "four letters") and correspond to the English YHWH. Based on Hebrew and Greek manuscripts, the most accurate transliteration of YHWH is "Yahweh". Jehovah is the name that is commonly used because someone substituted His real Name Yahweh for Jehovah. The fact remains that His authentic Name has been removed from most Bibles.

Bearing in mind that Yahweh's name has been replaced by LORD and or GOD, the entire Bible is replete with His Name. Most scriptures in the New Testament that are quoted from the Old Testament carry His Name. Let us have a look at some of them:

When Satan tempted Yeshua as narrated in Matthew 4, His response was: "It is written, Man does not live by bread only, but lives by every word that proceeds out of Yahweh's mouth (4). Further in verse 7 He said to Satan, again it is written, you shall not tempt Yahweh your God". His last response to Him was, "Get behind me Satan! For it is written "You shall fear Yahweh your God, and you shall serve Him, and you shall swear by His name" (Deuteronomy 8:3).

When Yeshua was teaching about the parable of the wicked vinedresser in Matthew 21:42, He said, "Have you not read in the Scriptures: "The stone which the builder rejected Has become the chief cornerstone. This was Yahweh's doing and it is marvellous in our eyes" (Psalm 118:22-23).

In Matthew 22, when responding to the group of Pharisees, He responded by quoting Psalm 110:1; He said: "Then how does David in the Spirit call Him Lord saying (43) Yahweh says to my Lord. Sit at My right hand, until I make Your enemies your footstool for your feet" (44).

When He lamented over Jerusalem in Matthew 23:39, He quoted Psalm 118:26: "For I tell you, you will not see Me from now on, until you say, Blessed is He who comes in Yahweh's Name".

In His response to one of the scribes who wanted to know which the greatest commandment of all is, Yeshua answered, "The greatest is commandment is "Hear O Israel: Yahweh is our God: Yahweh is one (Mark 12:29). You shall love Yahweh your God with all your heart, with all your soul, and with all you might (30). Same scripture as in Deuteronomy 6: 4 - 5.

In announcing His earthly ministry and His identity to His neighbours in Nazareth, He quoted Isaiah 61 as reflected in Luke 4, it reads: "The Lord Yahweh's Spirit is upon Me because Yahweh has anointed Me to preach the good news to the humble. He has sent Me to bind up the broken hearted. To proclaim liberty to the captives and release those who are bound. And recovery of sight to the blind (18). To proclaim the acceptable year of Yahweh's favour and the day of vengeance of our God" (19).

I concur with Snyder (2011) that the removal of Yahweh's name from the scriptures and from daily use by His people has serious implications. Yahweh tied His promises, His statutes, His covenants and salvation to His Name. The bottom line is that He wants His Name to be restored. Please note that it is not mandatory for anyone to call Him Yahweh. The assignment of this book is to restore His Name. He is Yahweh but you still have a choice.

> **God knows when we are addressing Him, so the name we use is unimportant.**

Yahweh delights at the mention of His Name. This truth has been hidden to many. Yahweh wants the eyes of our understanding to be opened. He desires His children to know who He is. Yahweh's word explicitly says, "My people are destroyed for lack of knowledge" (Hosea 4:6). Light shined in darkness, but darkness did not comprehend it. Yahweh wants us to call His Name. The Bible is abundant with instructions to declare His Name. For example, it commands us to shout His Name (Psalm 22:31), to proclaim His Name when we assemble together (Psalm 22:36), and to acknowledge His Name (Isaiah 26:13).

There is no harm in using His Name. It glorifies Him. Calling upon the Name of Yahweh is foundational to our salvation. The Bible tells us that whoever calls on the name of Yahweh shall be saved (Joel 2:32, Acts 2:21, and Romans 10:12). If the word says so, so it is, for the word of Yahweh is flawless. Proverbs 30:5 tells us that every word of Yahweh is pure. He is a shield to those who put their trust in Him. The verse that follows also cautions us to use His word with caution. It reads as follows: "Do not add to His Word lest He rebukes you and you are found to be a liar" (Proverbs 30:6).

> **Moses was the first person to use the Name Yahweh, so the Name itself is not eternal.**

Moses was not the first person to use the Name. Before Moses' existence, the Name of Yahweh was in use. The Bible tells us that after Seth begot Enosh, men started calling the Name of Yahweh (Genesis 4:26). This tells us that the Name was used before Moses' encounter with Yahweh at the burning bush. Furthermore, the compound titles were used before Moses' encounter with Yahweh at the burning bush. For example, Abraham called Him Yahweh Yireh (Genesis 22:14). Noah built an altar to Yahweh (Genesis 8:20), and Isaac built an altar and called on the Name of Yahweh (Genesis 26:25). Considering that the Name has been substituted with LORD O or GOD it suffices to say that the Name had been in use in the beginning of creation.

> **The Name Yahweh is not eternal**

This is another myth. Yahweh's name is eternal as His Godly being is. The eternal God who is Yahweh has always existed and continues to exist forever more. In Hebrew, His title that describes Him as eternal is El Olam, meaning forever, perpetual, implying that

He has an infinite future or past. Abraham also acknowledged Yahweh as eternal. Genesis 22:33 reads: "Abraham planted a tamarisk tree in Beersheba, and called the Name of Yahweh the everlasting God". Psalm 90:2 reads, "Before the mountains were born or you brought forth the earth and the world, from everlasting to everlasting you are God". Hosea 4:6 states that Yahweh's people are destroyed for lack of knowledge. This signifies a call to understand the power embedded in Yahweh, I AM THAT I AM. Bearing in mind that His Name has been substituted for LORD and GOD, the argument that Yahweh is not eternal falls way.

There is no reason whatsoever to prohibit us to use His name. He has used the foolish things of this world like me to restore His name. This is indeed provoking the Israelites to jealousy by the Gentiles. Let us call Him Yahweh and of course with reverence. It is now time to restore Yahweh's authentic Name. This is the time spoken by Yahweh in Zechariah 13:9 when He says: "I will bring the one third through the fire, will refine them as silver and test them as gold is tested, they will call upon My Name". When one has gone through Abba Father's furnace, they will not use His Name in vain but in honour and reverence. The next chapter attempts to explore the power in the Name of Abba Father, Yahweh.

FOUR

THE POWER IN
THE NAME YAHWEH

As mentioned in the previous chapter, Yahweh is the most powerful Name ever. The Name holds His eternal essence. It embraces His nature and significance. Yahweh is the Name that He revealed to us so we may know who He is. It carries the power of revelation and grace.

There is power in the Name Yahweh. Its meaning is so profound, although we know it in part. The part that He has revealed to us contains the power that is beyond our comprehension. I align myself to the meaning as given in rebjeff.com; it states that the Name Yahweh reveals His unchanging nature. It means that He is here, always has been and always will be. He is the sound purring past your ears that reassures you that no matter what you face, there is a reason for your existence.

There is a purpose for which you exist and you possess values that guide you to be the best you can be.

The name Yahweh points to Him as the Creator. The Name has also been interpreted as He who makes that which has been made and brings into existence that which exists (ancient eu.yahweh). The Bible is full of scriptures declaring Yahweh as the Creator. Nehemiah 6:9 reads: "You Yahweh, even You alone, You have made the heaven, the heaven with all their army, the earth and all things that are on it, the seas in all that is in them, and You preserve them. The army of heaven worship You".

The four letters that make the name Y-H-W-H (Yahweh) are all sounds. Yahweh is the sound of breathing. The Name Yahweh: יהוה is the sound of our breathing. It is the Spirit that was hovering over the waters. In Genesis 2:7, at creation, Yahweh breathes into us the breath of life. As long as we live we breathe in and out the Name of God. When we die, the Name leaves our bodies and we inert (Kohi, 2011).

I share the same sentiments with Kohi (2011) that Yahweh is a cosmic process operating throughout the dynamics laws of physics, chemistry and biology as well as covenantal companion. His Name reflects Him as the Holy One who listens and responds to our deepest personal yearnings.

The notion that Yahweh is the breath and the sound of the breath is well captured in Job. "But there is a spirit in man, and the breath of Almighty gives him understanding" (Job 32:8). "The Spirit of God has made gives me life" (Job 33:4). The breath of Yahweh is His creative power. Psalm 33:6 tells us that "By Yahweh's word, the heavens were made, all their armies by the breath of His mouth. Yahweh your Redeemer, and He who formed you from the womb says, "I am Yahweh, who makes all things, who alone stretches the heavens, who spread out the earth by Myself" (Isaiah 44:24).

His divine qualities are stressed in His Name. He is Yahweh our Maker (Psalm 94:6), He is Almighty (Psalm 80:19), He is the Most High (Psalms 7:17, 47:2-9) and our Judge. The book of Psalms is replete with His many attributes. In Psalm 24, He is revealed as the King of Glory. Some of His attributes are proclaimed in Exodus 6-7: "Yahweh passed before him, and proclaimed Yahweh! Yahweh, a merciful and gracious God, slow to anger, and abundant in loving kindness and truth. Keeping His loving kindness for thousands, forgiving inequity of fathers on the children, and on the children's children, on the fourth generation."

The Name Yahweh is far more powerful than what other religions call their version of the concept of God. It is the physical-word, equivalent to an esoteric and vibrational reality. It is an actual representation of the Universal Law that governs the primary pattern of all creation. The Name itself is the key to Creation and the representation of the Universal Law of polarities and the replication/reproduction of all vibration. Yahweh is the most significant metaphysical concept there is. It is the simplest thing in the universe, but perhaps the most difficult to really understand by the uninitiated and the uncircumcised.

The God of Abraham, the God of Isaac and the God of Jacob (Exodus 3: 6) is not His Name, thus Moses had a revelation that He should have a real Name. When God asked Moses to inform Pharaoh that God would extract the children of Israel out of Egypt (Exodus 3:10), Moses said to God, "Indeed if I go to the children of Israel and say to them. The God of your fathers has sent me to you and they say to me, what is His name, what shall I say to them?" Moses was not satisfied with God just being God of his fathers: the God of Abraham, the God of Isaac and the God of Jacob. Thanks to Moses who conversed with Yahuwah face-to-face and insisted on knowing His real identity.

The secret in the power of the Name Yahweh is embedded in the understanding of the Hebrew language and Yahuwah had not yet given me the gift to understand the language. I enrolled in Biblical Hebrew with the intention of learning more about His Name but that added to more confusion. In the two years of my Biblical Hebrew enrolment, His real Name Yahweh was never uttered. He was rather referred to as Adonai (ינודא) or Elohim (םיהולא).

I asked Yahweh to open the eyes of my understanding. He listened to my prayer and enlightened me. In my limited time of learning Biblical Hebrew, I learnt that literature started as pictures (pictographs). Each letter represents a symbol. Each symbol is a source of the wealth of the meaning attached to it. The word Yod was represented by a hand. The word heh means behold, while the letter vav refer to a hook or a nail.

The Name is represented by four letters in what is now known as the Hebrew alphabet, which have numerical as well as symbolical meanings. Important to note is that Hebrew was first written in symbol (s). It was first written down in consonants in 10th B.C.E, and vowels were added at a later stage. Significantly, the Name is actually far more ancient than the Hebrew symbols and alphabets.

Yod-He-Vav-He (YHVH) is allegedly pronounced 'Yod-Hay-Waw-Hey'. It is associated with the root word Heh-Yod – Hey (to be). It is known as Tetragrammaton. Tetragrammaton as already mentioned refers to a four letter word. Tetragrammaton signifies the infinite characteristics of the Creator.

The symbolic meaning of the name YHWH is as follows:

Y - Yod written as a symbol of a hand raised up.
H - hey – to be
W - Waw- or Vav- symbolised as a nail
H – hey-to be

Translated into English, YHWH with vowels added the name of God of the universe as Yahweh. Translated as I AM WHO I AM. I AM is the covenant name of Yahweh. Yahweh is the ultimate supreme being of the universe who is the Creator of all things. YHWH points exactly to the Creator. He is one without a second. His name is above all names. Yahweh is the Creator of all things and has made everything for His glory. The wealth of the name Yahweh is contained in the four letters YHWH. Some light on the weight of the letters YHWH has been shared in the previous chapters.

Together, the letters of YHWH's name unlock the mystery of salvation. For instance, Yod (y) – the hands, Hey (h) – behold, Wav (vav) – the nail, Hey h – behold! The word picture found in the Name of YHWH reveals the only path to eternal life. The Psalmist prophesied about the Saviour when he wrote that the Messiah's hands (yod) would be pierced by a nail (vav). Psalm 22 reads: "For dogs have surrounded Me. A company of evil doers have enclosed Me. They have pierced My hands and feet (16). I can count my bones. They look and stare at me (17) And they divide my garments among them. They cast lots for My clothing" (18).

Psalms 83:18 reads: "That people may know that you, whose name is Yahweh, You alone are the Most High over all the earth". The name Yahweh is best known for the famous "I AM" interaction with Moses (Exodus 3) and refers to the fact that God has always existed and will always exist. Though this is true, it is also a very basic understanding of the meaning of Yahweh. In the ancient world, names communicated something about a person's character, so a name carried much meaning with it. God in His infinite sovereignty chose to reveal Himself in the name Yahweh. Consequently, one should expect this name to communicate a lot about the character of Yahweh.

Yahweh is the Name that embraces all He is and what He is capable of. All the other titles emanate from His true name. The purpose of this book, as indicated earlier, is to restore His Name Yahweh. Literally, it gives us permission to call upon His Name. Nevertheless, we all have a choice to make, it is not compulsory. Yahweh exists and echoes in all spheres of life. He is the essence of all living beings; that is in human beings, the cosmos and in the world. His presence is in all that He created. In His dimension of human beings, He exists in both our bodies and lives. Thus, it is written: "For in

Him we live and have our being" (Acts 17: 28a). This is echoed in Psalm 24:1: "The earth is Yahweh's and all its fullness. The world and those who dwell therein".

Yahweh as reflected in the human body, the Yod is the head, the first "He" is the upper limbs and the Wav is the torso and the second "He" is the lower limbs. As reflected in human life, the Yod is the mind, the intellect, the first "He" is the emotions, the Waw is the life energy, the first He is the desire, the Waw is the animation, and the last "He" is the matter. As reflected in the cosmos, the Yod is the consciousness of creation, the first "He" is the impulse of creation, the Waw is the immaterial created universe, the second "He" is the material created universe (http:/shekinah. elysimgates.com /Hebrew.htm).

It is important to note that the time in which the Name Yahweh was suppressed, is sometime after the return of the children of Israel from their captivity in Babylon. It is before the beginning of the Christian era (approximately 310-199 B.C.E.). The victories of the Israelites could have been attributed by the use of His real Name Yahweh. Considering the period given to the prohibition of the Name, it means that until then, the prophets and in fact, all of Israel used the great Name Yahweh.

The children of Israel saw the power of the Name in action. They witnessed its power when He caused the ten plagues to liberate them from Pharaoh. It is the Name that delivered them from the hands of Pharaoh. They called on the Name when they walked through the waters of the Reed [2]Sea (Yam Suf). They saw the

2. Biblical Hebrew B: www.eTeacher Group.com

power of the Name when they ate manna which came directly from Yahweh. The Name has been the source of victory from their enemies. It has been the power behind Israel's ability to subdue nations. He has been Yahweh Tsavaot (God of Armies) in the history of Israel. It was only in turning from Yahweh to idolatry, as we are doing today, that caused Yahweh to hide His face from Israel and give their enemies advantage over them.

You and I are living under the grace of Yahweh and we are called to restore His name. There is power in the name of Yahweh. We are called to make His name known to all the earth. Yahweh desires that the eyes of our understanding be enlightened so that we become aware of the hope of His calling. What are the riches of His inheritance in the saints? (Eph. 1:18). Apostle Paul prayed that Yahweh of our Lord, Yeshua Christ and the Father of glory may give us the spirit of wisdom and revelation in the knowledge of Yahweh, the eyes of our understanding being enlightened that we may know what the hope of His calling is, what the glory of His inheritance in the saints is and what the exceeding greatness of His power towards us who believe is, according to the working of His mighty power (Eph. 1:18-19).

As we explore the Name Yahweh, I see the above scripture fulfilled. I am also reminded of the scripture in Deuteronomy 29:29: "The secret things belong to Yahweh, but the things which are revealed belong to us and our children forever, that we may do the words of this law". You and I are blessed; Yahweh wants us and our children to know Him.

Yahweh wants us to call Him by His Name. However, the scripture is so clear with the fact that He does not want us to use His Name in vain. Using the Name Yahweh in vain is about declaring what Yahweh has not said concerning us. For example, utterances such as I am poor, broke or useless, are a blasphemy to His Name. In Exodus 20:7 we are warned not to swear falsely by the His Name. Using His Name Yahweh in vain includes prophesying in His Name when He has not given us the prophecy, such actions are considered as profane to His Name (Leviticus 19:12, Jeremiah 29:9 and 21).

Yahweh's Name embraces all His attributes that pre-emanates Him apart as God. Some of His attributes are high-lighted in the next chapter. As you continue reading this book, you are reminded that it is an invitation for you to call upon His Name. You have a choice to accept or to decline the invitation just like those who were invited to the wedding feast in the parable in Matthew 22. I pray that Yahweh reveals Himself to you and that He increases your zeal for His knowledge. I also pray that Yahweh gives you the Spirit of wisdom and revelation that you may know that you may know him better (Ephesians.1:17).

Pronouncing the blessings in the Name of Yahweh releases His blessings upon us. The significance of releasing blessings in the name of Yahweh is reflected in Numbers 6:24-27 and reads as follows: "Yahweh bless you and keep you, Yahweh make His face shine upon you, and be gracious to you. Yahweh lift His countenance upon you and give you peace. So they shall put on My Name (Yahweh) and I will bless them". It gives instructions on how to pronounce blessings. When we bless somebody in the Name of Yahweh, we are putting His Name on them.

The Name of Yahweh is a seal that is put upon those who made their call and election sure. These are servants of Abba Father as indicated in Revelation 7: "Do harm neither the sea, nor trees, until we have sealed the bond servants of Yahweh on their foreheads" (3). Revelation 22 describes the River of Life and the servants of Yahweh. It is written: "The throne of Yahweh will be in it and His servants will serve Him (3). They will see His face and His name will be written on their foreheads" (4).

When we call upon the Name of Yahweh, accomplishment is ascertained. His Name is the actual release of power of whatever is being spoken. Yahweh is everything His children need. Yahweh wants His Name restored. Knowing His Name helps us understand His nature. Most of His titles tell us what he does or what He can do.

FIVE

YAHWEH'S NATURE

Yahweh is the ultimate supreme being of the universe. He is also the Creator of the world. YHWH points exactly to the Creator. He is one without a second. It is a Name above all names. Yahweh is the Creator of all things. He made everything for His glory. Our Yahweh is one. He is omnipotent, omnipresent and omniscient. He is all powerful, all present and all knowing. He desires that we know Him for who He is. All His aspects are embedded in His Name. The name-holder has some characteristic or descriptions that identify a person in question. This chapter highlights some of the attributes that are unique to Him as Yahweh.

YAHWEH IS THE CREATOR

The first chapter of Genesis accounts of creation and calls God Elohim, which means God in plural: God the

Father, the Son and the Holy Spirit. Genesis 2:4 introduces the covenant Name, Yahweh.[1] Here, this is combined with Elohim — YHWH-Elohim to show that the covenant God of Israel is none other than the Creator of the universe.

Other chapters in the Old Testament use God's covenant name (Yahweh) when they describe His creative work. For instance, Psalm 24 says: "The earth is Yahweh's and all its fullness, the world and those who dwell in it (1). For He has founded it upon the waters and established it upon the floods" (2). Isaiah 40 says: "we are called to acknowledge Yahweh as the Creator". It is written: "Lift up your eyes on high, and see who created these, who bring out by their army by number. He calls them all by name, by the greatness of His might, and because He is strong in power no one is lacking" (26).

In Yahweh all things were created: things in heaven and on earth, visible and invisible, whether thrones or powers, rulers or authorities; all have been created through Him and for Him (Col 1:16). The following scriptures attest to the fact that all things were created by Him:

By faith we understand that the universe was formed at God's command, so that what is seen was not made out of what was visible (Hebrews 11:13).

The God who made the world and everything in it, is the Lord of heaven and earth and does not live in temples built by human hands (Acts 17:24).

You are worthy, our Lord and God, to receive glory and honour and power, for you created all things, and by your will they were created and have their being (Revelation 7:12).

You alone are the LORD. You made the heavens, even the highest heavens, and their entire starry host, the earth and all that is on it, the seas and all that is in them. You give life to everything, and the multitudes of heaven worship you (Nehemiah 9: 6). Yahweh who made the earth, Yahweh who formed it to establish it. Yahweh is His name" (Jeremiah 33:2).

The Name Yahweh is the primary identifier of the true God. When Jonah wanted to identify himself with his God, he told the men on the ship that he was a Hebrew and that he feared God (Yahweh), the God of heaven who made the sea and the dry land (Jonah 1:9). This knowledge was not limited to the Hebrews; Hiram the king of Tyre in Solomon's days, recognised that the God of Israel, was the Creator: "Blessed is Yahweh God of Israel, who made heaven and earth" (2 Chronicles 2:12).

"Thus says Yahweh, who gives the sun for light by day and the fixed order of the moon and stars for light by night, who stirs up the sea so that its waves roar, Yahweh of hosts is His name" (Jeremiah 31:35, Zechariah 12:1). In actual fact, the entire universe is a magnificent display of the splendour of the glorious Creator, Yahweh. The wonder of creation is so awesome to behold. The universe, as created by Yahweh reflects harmony, consistency and elegance. Because Yahweh created the world, He has the authority and the power to make sure that His word is fulfilled. We therefore should reverence Him. He alone is Yahweh. No one else is even near qualified to create a secondary position to Him. He is the Supreme Being. What we called discovery in nature, He has created. The word discovers does not apply to Him. Yahweh, as the Creator is the giver of life. This next section discusses Him as life.

YAHWEH, AS THE CREATOR, IS LIFE

He is the giver of life to all creation. He does not only give life but He is life itself. Without His breath, nothing that is alive could be alive. Yahweh creates and gives life. He is the source of life for all He has created, both visible and invisible. He is life, nothing lives outside Him. Life is an enduring paradox and so is Yahweh. All we know about Him is that He is self-existent, how He became is beyond our comprehension. Life as Yahweh is more of a spiritual essence besides His physical existence. Genesis 2:7 says: "And Yahweh God formed men of the dust of the ground , and breathed into the nostrils the breath of life , and men became a living being". Yahweh expressing Himself as the Life Giver says: "See now that I, I am He, And there is no god besides Me; It is I who put to death and give life I have wounded and it is I who heal, And there is no one who can deliver from My hand" (Deuteronomy 32:40).

Job also acknowledged Yahweh as the source of life when he expressed himself thus: "Who does not know that in all these, Yahweh's hand has done this? In whose hands is the life of every living thing, and the breath of all mankind?" (Job 12:10). When the children of Israel were confessing their sins to Yahweh they also prayed and said "You alone are Yahweh, You have made the heavens. The heaven of heavens with their entire host, the earth and everything on it. And you preserve them all. The hosts of heaven worship You" (Nehemiah 9:6). According to John 1: 18, no one has seen Yahweh, yet we are all witnesses of His capabilities. We live and have our being in Him. Our Creator as Light and Life is one. The next section focuses on Yahweh's nature as the only God.

YAHWEH IS ONE

The scriptures affirm that Yahweh is one and that there is none like Him (Det. 4:35, 6:34, 39 1 Tim 2:5, Nehemiah 9:6). There is none like him and there is no other God (Isaiah 43:10 -11). His oneness is emphasised in many scriptures, for example, Yahweh introduces Himself as the only Yahweh. Besides Him there is no other (Isaiah 45: 5, 14, 21 and 46: 9). He further states that before Him there was no God nor shall be God after Him (not only is He one but He is Yahweh of the kingdoms of all the earth, 2 Kings 19:15).

Yeshua also emphasised that Yahweh is one. When the scribes asked Him what the most important commandment is, He quoted Deuteronomy 6:4: "The foremost is, 'hear, o Israel! The Lord our God is one Lord; and you shall love the Lord your God with all your heart, and with all your soul, and with your entire mind, and with all your strength" (Mark 12:28-30). We also observe how He made a declaration that Yahweh is one when He was praying to Abba Father for Himself. Yeshua said, "This is eternal life, that they may know You, the only true God, and Jesus Christ whom You have sent" (John 17:3). Yahweh deserves the entire honour, all the glory and all the praise as our one and only God. He is worthy of all praise. Our only Yahweh calls us to worship Him in Spirit and in truth. He abides in the praises of His people.

Important to note is that even though Yahweh is one, He is also Trinity. Yahweh is one: Yahweh the Father, Yahweh the Son and Yahweh the Holy Spirit. In John 10:30 Yeshua affirms His intricacy with Yahweh when He says "I and the Father are one". In John 14 when He revealed the Father to His disciples, He emphasised the oneness of God. He says: "Do you not know that I am the Father and the Father in Me? The word that I speak to you, I do not speak on your own authority, but the Father that dwells in e does the works (10). Believe Me that I am in the Father, and the Father is me, or else believe e for the sake of the works themselves". The intricacy of the Father and the Son makes it difficult to talk about their attributes independently. What Yahweh is, so is His Son. Not only is Yahweh one, He is also great. The nest section highlights His greatness.

YAHWEH IS GREAT

He is so great that no one can fathom His greatness. Yahweh is great in who He is and in His actions. The greatness of Yahweh refers to Him as all powerful. His title that describes His greatness is "El Gadol (the Great God). The Bible is abundant with His greatness. Psalm 95:3 referring to His greatness reads, "For Yahweh is a great God, a great King above all gods". All power belongs to Him. The Bible tells us that our Yahweh is the great God. Yahweh is the great and awesome God. Yahweh's greatness is explicitly expressed in Exodus 15:11: "Who is like You, O Yahweh among the gods, who is like you glorious in holiness, fearful in praise, doing wonders".

The description of Yahweh in Deuteronomy 10:17 is phrased this way, "You shall not be terrified of them, for the Yahweh your God, the great and awesome God is among you. And for the Lord our Yahweh is the God of gods, and the Lord of Lords, the Great God, mighty and awesome, who shows no partiality nor takes a bribe".

When Nehemiah prays for his nation, he addresses Yahweh as follows: "Yahweh God of heaven, great and awesome Yahweh (1:5a). He further refers to Him as the great, the mighty and awesome God (Nehemiah 9: 2 & 23). The psalmists in Psalm 68:35 and 147:5 attests to the greatness and awesomeness of God. Psalm 68:35 says: "Oh God you are more awesome than your holy places" (Psalm 68:35) and Psalm 147 reads: "Great is our Yahweh, and mighty in power, His understanding is infinite".

His greatness is far beyond any imagination. It is indescribable and unsearchable. If heaven is His throne and the earth His footstool, then He has the depth of the earth in His hand. No wonder Job asked his friends if they can fathom the mysteries of Yahweh or probe His limits (Job 11:7). He's so great in all He is and in all that He does.

One day during a church service, the congregation was singing the song "How great is our God", I closed my eyes and asked Him to show me how great He is. He showed me a vision of what I thought could be a moon or sun. Throughout the service, all I could see was that object. The same evening, a neighbour's son came and asked to watch a video with us. Little did I know that his visit was more of an answer to the vision I had while I was in the church. What I saw was neither the moon nor the sun but it was a star. I did not know that the tiny, shining dots that shine at night were that big. Picturing that one star is the size of Africa; it is imaginable how big our Yahweh is. The little stars that we see in the sky are mere dots on the cosmos, yet Yahweh knows them by name. The video pointed to Yahweh as indescribable and uncontainable. He places the stars in the sky, and He knows them by name. He is awesome.

We are too small; we are like grains of sand to Him, yet He cares for us and made us to be gods. Psalm 145:3 captures Yahweh's greatness so well, it reads: "Great is Yahweh and greatly to be praised and His greatness is unsearchable". Indeed, Yahweh is great in all He is, in faithfulness, in His works, in His love, in His mercy, and in His grace. In Job 36:26, Elihu, Job's friend says of Yahweh, "How great is God — beyond our under-standing! The number of His years is past finding out". Similarly, Psalms 95:1–5 and 96:1–6 call us to worship Him for His greatness.

Yahweh is great, but He is not too great to miss you in the crowd. He knows the exact number of your hairs on your head. His sight never loses sight of us. With Yahweh is always perfect vision. He says, "See I have engraved you on the palms of My hands. Your walls are always before Me" (Isaiah 49:16). He is great, yet closer than our next breath. Yahweh's greatness also manifests in His power. Powerfulness is His nature.

YAHWEH IS OMNIPOTENT

Yahweh is infinite power. He is truly all powerful. His power is exercised effortlessly. The indescribable power of Yahweh is so evident in Genesis 1 when He spoke and created all things in heaven and above and in all earth below. He is omnipotent beyond human understanding. Often, when I watch television and see natural catastrophes: floods, storms and volcanoes, I wonder how powerful Yahweh is. His power is not only displayed in natural disasters but in all His creation.

The Bible gives some great descriptions and verses on Yahweh's great power. His nature was powerfully displayed when He conquered battles for the children of Israel. For example, Exodus 17:8 -13 gives an account of how Joshua had victory over the Amalekites. David prevailed against Goliath because he did not use his strength. He used Yahweh's Name. A narration of David and Goliath is given in 1 Samuel 17. Verse 45 reads: "Then David said to the Philistine, You come to me with a sword, with a spear, and with Javelin. But I came to you in the name of Yahweh of hosts, the God of armies of Israel, whom you have defiled". In 2 Chronicles 20:14-27 we read about how Jehoshaphat defeated the Ammon and Moab at Mount Seir. Psalm 136 gives a snapshot of Yahweh's power. Yahweh is mighty in battles. He does whatever pleases Him. Psalm 147:5 describes Him as great and mighty in power. Not only is He powerful in battles but also in His word, which He carries through His powerful voice. He is powerful in His thoughts and actions. Taking into consideration that Yahweh is powerful, nothing is too hard for Him, nothing is too difficult for Him and that what is humanly impossible is possible with Him. This should be a motivation for us to be deeply grounded in Him.

HE IS POWERFUL IN HIS WORD

Omnipotent as He is, we should take note that He magnifies His word above His Name (Psalm 138:2). Hebrews 4: 12 tells us that "The word of Yahweh is living and active, sharper than any double-edged sword, piercing even to the division of soul and spirit, and of the joints and marrow and is discerner of thoughts and intents of the heart. Knowing for sure that the power in His word is limitless we tap into it at any time we find ourselves in powerless situations. His word is constant. Psalm 119:89 tells us that His word stands forever, it reads: "Forever, Oh Yahweh, Your word is settled in heaven".

Yeshua Himself declared that heaven and earth will pass away, but His words will never pass away (Matthews 24:35 and Luke 21:33). The least we can do is to meditate on the word and believe in its power as we communicate to Yahweh and to one another. Speaking the word is the power of Christ like life to all believers. The scripture exhorts us to let the word to dwell in us so that we speak to one another in psalms and hymns, and spiritual songs and making melody to

Yahweh (Ephesians 5 19 and Colossians 3:16) and that our speech should always be with grace, seasoned with salt, so that we may know how to answer one another (Colossians 4:6). The victory for believers lies in realising the power of His word and speaking it.

YAHWEH IS POWERFUL IN HIS VOICE

Psalm 29:3-9 tells us about the power of the voice of Yahweh. It tells us that, "The voice of Yahweh is over the waters, the voice of Yahweh is full of majesty, that it thunders, it breaks the cedars of Lebanon and makes them also skip like a calf, divides the flames of fires, shakes the wilderness of Kadesh, makes the deer give birth and strips the forest bare and His temple everyone says Glory"!

Although Yahweh is all powerful, His desire is for His children to revere Him rather than being too afraid of Him. He is Abba Father who delights in fellowshipping with Him. His love for us endures forever and He loves all His children unconditionally. Yahweh cares so much about us. He is concerned and has interest in our affairs. He cares to such an extent that He even knows the number of our hair (Matthew 10:30 and Luke 12:14). When there is need for discipline; He really applies the corrective measures. He disciplines those whom He loves. Proverbs 3 reads, "My son do not despise the chastening of Yahweh nor detest His correction (12). For whom Yahweh loves He corrects, just as a father the son in whom he delights" (13). He is not like some natural fathers who are alienated to their children as they are so hard on them by emotionally or physically abusing their children. All He requires from us is to use His name in reverential fear. His is not abusive in His power.

Yahweh wants us to worship Him for whom He is: Abba Father, the Father who loves unconditionally and disciplines where necessary. I had a good loving father, who would play with my siblings and I. If you disobeyed the rules, you were definitely sure that you would get a hiding. I am sharing this because I believe that this is the kind of relationship that Yahweh wants us to have with Him. Unlike our earthly fathers, Yahweh is continuously watching over us. There is nothing that is hidden before Him because of His nature as omnipresent.

YAHWEH IS OMNIPRESENT

Yahweh is invisible for He is Spirit. In as much as we do not see Him, He is everywhere all the time. Yahweh continuously watches over mankind. Through His Spirit that dwells with us, He is continually with us as individuals. In Psalms 14:2, we are told that Yahweh looks down from heaven upon the children of men to see if there is any who understands and who seeks Him.

No one can run from the presence of Yahweh. If we miss the mark and do what is evil before His eyes, He says to us: "If my people who are called by My name, will humble themselves, and pray and seek My face, and turn from their wicked ways, then I will hear from heaven and heal their land. Now My eyes will be open and my ears will be attentive to prayer made in this place. For now, I have chosen and sanctified this house that My name may be with them forever, and my eyes and heart will be there perpetually" (2 Chronicles 7: 14-16). Oh! What a blessing to have Yahweh's eyes and heart to be with us forever. His omnipresence calls us to run to him and not away like Jonah did.

The Psalmist (Psalm 139) captures the omnipresence of Yahweh when He says: "Where can I go from Your Spirit? Or where can I flee from Your presence? If I ascend to heaven, You are there; If I make my bed in Sheol, behold, You are there. If I take the wings of the dawn, if I dwell in the remotest part of the sea". He is indeed everywhere at the same time.

This is evident as captured in (Jeremiah 23:23-24). Yahweh declares that He is a God at hand and not far off. No man can hide from Him. Implied is that He sees man in his hiding place. Referring to His omnipresence, He says that He fills the earth. Nothing is hidden from His sight. Daniel 2:22 says, "It is He who reveals the profound and hidden things. He knows what is in the darkness. And the light dwells with Him". It is His light that exposed deep and hidden things. Everything is laid bare before Him.

Yahweh's eyes range to and from the earth (2 Chronicles 16:19 and Zechariah 4:10). In Him we live and have our being. This is an indication that we exist in Him. He is in our midst. He is always present wherever we are. Nothing in our lives and in the universe takes Him by surprise. He knows our beginning from the end, for He is knowledge. Intertwined with His nature as omnipresent is that He is eternal.

YAHWEH IS ETERNAL AND ETERNITY IS YAHWEH'S NATURE

He is not defined by time. Time exists in Him. He is from everlasting to everlasting. He has no beginning and He has no end. He is eternal in all His attributes. He is not a succession of moments. He is constant in His time. He is the same, yesterday, today and forever. The Bible is full of Yahweh's word about His eternity. Some of the passages that relate to Yahweh's eternity include:

Psalm 90:1 reads: "Yahweh you have been our dwelling place to His eternity in all generations. Before the mountains were brought forth. Or even You had formed the earth and the world. Even from everlasting to everlasting You are Yahweh".

Psalm 45:6 and 93:2 and 5, refer to His throne as everlasting. Psalm 45: 6 reads: "Your throne O Yahweh is forever, the sceptre of righteousness is the sceptre of your Kingdom", and Psalm 93:2 and 6 talks of His eternal throne, His testimonies that are very sure and the holiness that adorns His house forever.

YAHWEH IS ETERNAL IN HIS WORD

His word is forever settled in heaven. His promises are yes and amen. Yahweh is eternal in His attributes. His love, mercy, kindness and faithfulness endure forever; Yahweh inhibits eternity. What Yahweh does is everlasting. Nothing shall be added to it, and nothing shall be taken from it. Yahweh is eternal. We should therefore revere Him. Just look at the sun, the moon, the stars, the mountains and the seas. They stand forever.

YAHWEH IS OMNISCIENT

Yahweh is knowledge. He possesses all the knowledge of everything that one can think of. His knowledge is perfect and limitless. There is no end to it. He does not need to learn anything. He is the creator of all things visible and invisible. Yahweh does not have "I do not know" in His vocabulary. Things that take human beings to learn through a microscope are laid bare before His eyes. Daniel 2:21 talks about Yahweh as knowledgeable, it says: "He reveals deep secret things, He knows what is in darkness and light dwells with Him".

I stand in awe of Yahweh when I try to meditate on Him as omniscient. Let us have a look at what He says of Himself, He says in Isaiah 46, "I declare the end from the beginning, and the ancient things that are yet to be done (9). I say y counsel will stand and I will do as I please (10). No one has indeed Yahweh's Spirit or taught Him as His counselor. He is indeed knowledge. His omniscient nature is reiterated in Isaiah 40:13 and says: "Who did He take counsel with, and also instructed Him, and taught Him path of justice, and taught Him knowledge, and showed Him the way of understanding".

The reality that Yahweh is knowledge has been acknowledged by Job in several scriptures. For example, Job 21:22 says, "Can anyone teach knowledge to God, since He judges even the highest". Further in 37:16 Job says, "Do you know how the clouds hang poised, those wonders of Him who has perfect knowledge"?

His knowledge is beyond human comprehension. The Bible tells us that "He determines the number of the stars and calls them each by name. Great is our Lord and mighty in power; His understanding has no limit" (Psalm 147:4). His limitless knowledge is summed up in Romans 11:33: "Oh, the depth of the riches of the wisdom and knowledge of God. How unsearchable his judgments, and His paths beyond tracing out".

Yahweh does not discover anything. All things are His. He created all visible and invisible things, both great and small. He is Yahweh of all creation. The first chapter of the Bible gives a good narration of how He created all that He created. It is interesting to note that Yahweh has knowledge about you and me. He knows our thoughts and our movements. He even directs our steps. Psalm 139:1–5 outlines His knowledge of human nature. His thoughts are higher than our thoughts. He is incredibly wise; there is no wisdom outside Him — for He is wisdom. Scriptures referring to His wisdom say:

"There is no wisdom and no understanding and no counsel against Yahweh" (Proverbs 21: 30). His wisdom is beyond the wisdom of philosophers of this age. His wisdom frustrates the wise of this world. It is by His wisdom, knowledge and understanding that all things are created (Proverbs 3:19).

1 Corinthians 1:20: "Where is the wise man? Where is the scribe? Where is the philosopher of this age? Has not God made foolish the wisdom of the world?"

1 Corinthians 3:18–19: "Let no one deceive himself, if anyone among you seems to be wise in this age, let he

become a fool that he may be wise. For the wisdom of this world is foolishness with Yahweh. For He catches the wise in their craftiness".

Yahweh is knowledgeable. His insight and counsel are beyond any human comprehension. The Bible tells us that His ways are higher than our ways and His thoughts higher than ours. Romans 11 sums it very well: "Oh, the depth of the riches and wisdom and knowledge of God (33), how unsearchable are His judgments and how inscrutable His ways (34). For who has known the mind of the LORD, or who has been His counselor? Or who has given a gift to Him that He might be repaid? (35). For from Him and through Him and to Him are all things. To Him be glory forever, Amen" (36).

In Isaiah 40:28, there is proof of how knowledgeable Yahweh is, Isaiah says, "Have you not known? Have you not heard? The Lord is the everlasting God, the Creator of the ends of the earth. He does not faint or grow weary; his understanding is unsearchable". Daniel 2:22 gives a good description of how knowledgeable Yahweh is. He says ". He reveals deep and hidden things; He knows what lies in darkness, and light dwells with Him.

Yahweh is not selfish with His Knowledge and does not desire that His children be ignorant. His desire is that we become knowledgeable. In Hosea 4:6a we read, "My people are destroyed for lack of knowledge". Psalm 19: 2 tells that day unto day utters speech and night after night He reveals knowledge. As Alpha and Omega, He knows the beginning from the end. This is well captured in Isaiah 46:10: "I make known the end from the beginning, from ancient times, what is still to come I say my purpose will stand; I will do all that I please". He is not surprised by events.

Integrated in His nature as omniscient, are His divine qualities of truth and faithfulness. What He has made known to us remains. He does not change His mind. He is faithful to His word. Forever His word is settled in heaven and His faithfulness endures to all generations. In Matthew 12: 13, 24: 35 and Luke 21:33, Yeshua says, "Heaven and earth will pass away, but my words will by no means pass away". Isaiah 40:8 says "The grass withers and the flowers fades, but the word of Yahweh stands forever". Fashion will come and go but His word stands forever. The word of Yahweh is truth (John 17: 17b).

Who has known the mind of Yahweh or has been His counselor? Indeed, His understanding is unsearchable. The absolute truth about Yahweh as knowledge is well phrased in Romans 11:33, it reads: "Oh the depth of the wisdom and knowledge of Yahweh. How unsearchable His judgments, and his paths beyond tracing out".

He is wisdom. Yahweh is all wise, infinitively wise. When I visualise how He created the creation, the ark, the Tabernacle, and us as human beings and how our bodies function, I stand in awe of His wisdom. Look around and picture the beauty of His creation and that will give you a glimpse of His wisdom.

It is interesting to note that the all-knowing Yahweh is interested in the affairs of His children. He cares about us. He knows everything concerning us. There is nothing that surprises Him concerning our lives. He knows our thoughts and our ways. Some passages in the Bible that attest to that include:

- For His eyes are upon the ways of man, He sees all his steps (Job 34:21).
- For man's ways are before the eyes of Yahweh and He observes all his path (Proverbs 5:21).
- Can anyone hide himself in places so secret that I will not see him? Do I not fill heaven and earth? It is the declaration of Yahweh (Jeremiah 23:24).
- Matthew 10: Are not two sparrows sold for a penny? Yet not one of them will fall to the ground apart from the will of your Father (29.) And even the very hairs of your head are all numbered (30).
- Indeed, the very hairs of your head are all numbered. Don't be afraid; you are worth more than many sparrows (Luke 12:7).
- Whenever our hearts condemn us. For God is greater than our hearts, and He knows everything (1 John 3:20).

To sum it up, Yahweh is indescribable and uncontainable. Yahweh is the most valuable reality and Spirit being in the universe. He is more worthy of interest, attention, admiration, and enjoyment than all other realities, including the entire universe.

YAHWEH IS OMNIPOTENT

Yahweh is all powerful. He is unlimited in power. He is immeasurably powerful God. Some of His attributes as powerful have been highlighted under chapter four. He has many titles that describe His nature as all power-ful. He is Yahweh Elshaddai (Almighty: Genesis 17:1).

Yahweh Tsevaot (God of Armies), El Gibbor (God Almighty or My Mighty Helper, Genesis 17, Psalm 65:6, Jeremiah 32:17). Yahweh Elyon (the Most High, Psalm 47:2), El Gomer (Yahweh who performs, Psalm 57:2) and Yahweh Sali (God our fortress, Jeremiah 16:19). His omnipotence is well captured in Job 38-39. In His conversation and questions to Job, He emphasises that He is the Creator of all things visible and invisible. In the same conversation, He also brings His nature as Almighty. In His power, Yahweh performs miracles that cannot be countered and wonders that cannot be fathomed. Yahweh does whatever He pleases. He is always right, always beautiful, always faithful, always wonderful, always merciful, always truthful and in accord with His word. Most importantly, He is utterly free from any constraint.

Yahweh is never constrained to do a thing that He despises. He is never backed into a corner where His only recourse is to do something He hates to do. He has pleasure in all that He does. He always acts in freedom, according to His own good pleasure, following the dictates of His own delights (Pipe, 2019). Yahweh never becomes the victim of circumstance. He is never forced into a situation where He must do something in which He cannot rejoice. He is not mocked. He is not trapped or cornered or coerced.

Psalm 115:3 reads: "Our God in heaven does what He pleases". Whatever Yahweh pleased, that He has done in heaven and in earth, in the sea and all the deeps (Psalm 135:6). Yahweh declared Himself as powerful to Pharaoh, and He said, "But indeed for this purpose I have raised you up, that I may show My power in you, and that My name may be declared in all the earth" (Romans 9:17 citing Exodus 9:16).

Yahweh is absolute wisdom, knowledge, insight and understanding. His understanding is infinite. Yahweh is the absolute standard of truth, goodness and beauty. There is no law-book to which He looks to know what is right and no almanac to establish facts. There is no guild to determine what is excellent or beautiful. He Himself is the standard of what is right, what is true and what is beautiful. Yahweh never has a beginning. He always existed and He always will. He is and who is to come, He is existent and all things exist in Him. Yahweh will never have an end. His existence will never go out of existence because He is and will always be.

Yahweh is absolute reality, there is no reality before Him, there is no reality outside of Him unless He wills and makes it. He is all that is eternal. He is not bound by time; time exists in Him. Only in Him there is all reality which is outside of him. He created, designed and governs as the absolute reality. He is utterly free from any constraints that do not originate from the counsel of His own will.

Yahweh is utterly independent. He depends on nothing, yet everything that is not Him depends totally on Him. The entire universe is secondary. It came into being through Him and stays in being moment by moment through His decision to keep it being.

Yahweh is constant. He is the same yesterday, today and forever. He cannot be improved. He is not becoming anything. He is who He is and who He says He is.

Yahweh, who is our Father in heaven, abides in the praises of His people and He wants His Name restored. Knowing His Name helps us to understand His nature. Most of what we call His names are His titles (Snyder, 2011). Most of His titles inform us of what He is capable of doing and that is beyond measure.

Apostle Paul prayed that the God of our Lord Yeshua Christ, the Father of glory may give us the spirit of wisdom and revelation in the knowledge of Yahweh. He prayed for the eyes of our understanding to be enlightened so that we may know what the hope of His calling, the glory of His inheritance in the saints and what the exceeding greatness of His power towards us who believe, according to the working of His mighty power is (Eph.1:18–19).

As we explore the name Yahweh, I see the above scripture fulfilled. I am also reminded of the scripture in Deut. 29:29, it reads: "The secret things belong to Yahweh, but the things which are revealed belong to us and our children forever, that we may do the words of this law". You and I are blessed. Yahweh wants us and our children to know Him.

Yahweh is eternal and is enthroned above the highest reach of the cosmos. Heaven is His throne and the earth is His footstool. Yahweh in His greatness cares for us. He has engraved us in the palm of His hands. He hides us under the tabernacle of His wings. He cares to the extent that He knows the number of hairs on your head. Yahweh is great and His greatness cannot be fathomed. He is aware of the smallest details of your life. Yahweh is so concerned about us that even before we pray, He answers our prayers.

The least we can do for Yahweh is to exalt His Name and glorify Him for who He is. Yahweh wants us to call upon His name. He is the only true God. It is written: "Yet to us there is but one God, the Father, of whom are all things, and we for Him; and one Lord, Yeshua Ha Mashiach, through whom all things, and we live through Him" (1 Corinthians 8:6, NLT).

All aspects of life are in His Name, they are embraced in His Name, His nature, His attributes, His capabilities and His purpose for all of us. I have stated that all aspects of life, religion and science are embodied in the Name YHWH. He is limitless in all He is. He is far beyond any imagination. He is indescribable, He is our great God.

Yahweh talks to the message of the cross. Yahweh is a merciful God, mainly because He sent His son Yeshua to forgive the sins of humanity. Despite His creation's repeated disobedience, Yahweh has shown mercy to us by giving us permission to call upon His Name.

At this point I would like to ask you if you have received Yeshua Ha Mashiach as your personal Lord and Saviour. In John 5 He says of Himself: "I have come in My Father's name, and you do not receive Me If another comes in his own name, him you will receive" (43). How can you believe, who receive glory from one another, and do not seek the glory that comes from the only God" (44). This is the time to accept He who comes in the Name of Yahweh and turn away from those who come in their own names.

The book of Genesis' accounts of creation calls God Elohim, a more generic name, however Genesis 2:4 introduces the covenant Name, Yahweh.[1] Here, this is combined with Elohim — YHWH-Elohim — to show that the covenant God of Israel is none other than the creator of the universe. Other places in the Old Testament use God's covenant Name, Yahweh, when they describe His creative work, for instance, Yahweh who made the earth, Yahweh who formed it to establish it —Yahweh is His Name (Jeremiah 33:2). This is a primary identifier of the true God. When Jonah wants to identify himself and his God, he tells the men on the ship, "I am a Hebrew, and I fear Yahweh, the God of heaven, who made the sea and the dry land" (Jonah 1:9). And this knowledge was not limited to the Hebrews: Hiram the king of Tyre in Solomon's day recognised that Israel's God was the Creator: He said; "Blessed is Yahweh God of Israel, who made heaven and earth" (2 Chronicles 2:12).

When scripture emphasises the authority of Yahweh's words, the prophets often appeal to God's creative power. For example, Jeremiah says: "God has made the earth by His power. He has established the world by His wisdom and by His understanding He stretched out the heavens (10:12). When He utters His voice, the waters in the heaven roar, and He causes the vapour to ascend from the ends of the earth. He makes lightning for rain, and brings the wind out of His chambers, and brings the wind of His treasures". Thus says Yahweh, who gives the sun for light by day and the fixed order of the moon and stars for light by night, who stirs up the sea so that its waves roar — Yahweh of hosts is His name" (Jeremiah 31:35, Zechariah 12:1).

As I conclude this chapter, I want to emphasise that Yahweh exists outside time, space and matter because He created time, space and matter. He does not exist in a specific place, He is everywhere. He does not exist somewhere in this universe; the universe exists somewhere within Him. He is not subject to time; He is simultaneously in all times: past, present and future.

Even though as humankind, we understand Him in minute fractions, He has attributes that we can relate to. Taking into consideration of how His attributes are as infinite as He is, the next chapter looks at some of them.

SIX

YAHWEH'S ATTRIBUTES

Yahweh has many attributes that are unique to Him, to mention a few, He is love, peaceful, joy, merciful, faithful, trustworthy, glorious, slow to anger, holy, good, marvellous, wonderful, and light. In other words, He is perfect in all His ways. This chapter focuses on His following attributes namely, light, love and holiness.

YAHWEH IS LIGHT

No one on the earth knows what light is. We know it moves in waves and we know that it is made up of particles. We also know that particles cannot move in waves and that waves cannot contain particles. However, that's not what light is; because whatever light is, Yahweh is. He spoke and light became. Light is Yahweh's existence and it is Yahweh's first creation.

Only Him knows how dark the darkness was before He spoke light into being. Light is not easy to comprehend. It appears to be both a particle and a wave, which of course, is impossible. Light is the fastest known quantity in the universe. It is able to be in two places at once.

Light travels across unimaginable eons of time and space to show us the far reaches of our universe and even the distance past it. Yahweh is light, He occupies the entire universe. Generally, we do not see light; however, we see through it, we actually see everything else through the reflection of light. Yahweh is Spirit and those who believe in Him must believe that He is. He is our Spiritual Light and through Him, as Light, our inner man is illuminated, giving us a deeper revelation of who He is, and eventually leading us into His truth.

The word from the mouth of Yahweh created light. The wonderful thing about this is how Yahweh created light in the midst of heaven and earth where the Spirit of Yahweh was hovering over the waters. I can only imagine how darkness was over the surface of the deep before Yahweh spoke light forth and it became.1 John 1:5b tells us that Yahweh is light. I AM THAT I AM is light, and in Him there is no darkness at all.

He is light and before Yahweh spoke light into existence, He was light. 1 John 1:5 tells us that: "This is the message that we had from Him and announce to you that Yahweh is light". Light is the first creation that Yahweh spoke and it came into being. Yahweh reproduces, replicates, or extends from Himself the light that He is. He speaks and so it is. If you are scientific, you could consider this process as cloning. Yahweh basically cloned Himself and brought forth the light so that you and I can see. He spoke His presence into existence. The word from the mouth of Yahweh spoke light to become. Interesting to note is that light, like human beings, is created in four dimensions. Let us examine these dimensions:

Firstly, He spoke and light became: "Let there be light and there was light" (Genesis 1:3). After He spoke light came into being, the Bible tells us that it was good. In Genesis 1:2-5, the word light appears five times. Five is the numerical value of the letter "hey". Light as an attribute of Yahweh reflects salvation. It also includes all the other aspects of the letter "Hey". It is through light that we get the revelation of Yahweh.

Secondly, He separated the light from a phenomenon known as darkness. He called the light Day and the darkness He called Night. Now that there was evening and morning, it became known as the first day (Genesis 1:4). The word "day" in scripture is used in three ways:

1. As a part of the day which consists of twenty-four hours, which is light;
2. As such days are set apart for distinctive purpose, for example, a day of atonement, a Sabbath day; and
3. A period of time, long or short, which reveals Yahweh's purposes which are to be accomplished, such as the day of the Lord.

The use of night may be to limit the full essence of the sun. It can refer to each creative day as a period of time marked off by beginning and ending.

Thirdly, He prophesied light to be in firmament with the heavens. Genesis 1:14 reads as follows: "Then Yahweh said, let there be lights in the firmament of the heavens to divide the day from the night and let them be for signs for seasons and for days and years. And let them be in the firmament of the heavens to give light on the earth and it was so".

Fourthly, Yahweh made two great lights, the greater light to rule the day and the lesser light to rule the night. He also made the stars (Genesis 1:16). Yahweh set them in the firmament with the heavens, to give light and to rule over the day and over the night — to divide the light from darkness (Genesis 1:16-17). I personally liken the greater light to Yeshua Ha Mashiach as He is depicted in Malachi 4:3a; it reads: "But to you who fear my name shall the Sun of Righteousness arise with healing its wings".

In all His creation, it is only the light that He designed to mark seasons, days and years and to rule over the day and night. Of all that He created in four dimensions; human beings and light are the ones that He also allotted authority. As human beings, Yahweh gave us authority as it appears in Genesis 1:28: "Yahweh blessed and said be fruitful and multiply, fill the earth and subdue it, have dominion over the fish of the sea, the birds of the air, and over every living thing that moves on the earth".

Noticeably, Yahweh did not give mankind dominion to rule over the light that He created. He Himself is light and mankind is subject to Him. A vessel cannot have dominion over the potter who made it. We are minute lights, yet very significant minute lights in His eyes.

There are a lot of scriptures that give the description of Yahweh as light. Following are some of the scriptures:

- Habakkuk 3:4: His brightness was like light. He had rays of flashing from His hand and there His power was hidden. Yahweh is light and dwells in unapproachable light. The light of Yahweh is likened to His glory.
- Isaiah 9:2 proclaims: The people who walked in darkness, have seen a great light. Those who dwell in the land of the shadow of death upon them a light has shined.
- In John 8:12, Yeshua identifies Himself as the light of the world and that whoever follows Him will never walk in darkness but will have the light of life.

The description of Yahweh as the light reveals Him as the Manifesto. He is the One who shines and makes things visible. Just as physical light does, He also enables us to see, so that we might walk confidently and find what we seek. All things are made to manifest by the light. Let us look at Yahweh as love.

Yahweh is Love. Love is more of the essence of Yahweh than His other attributes. The Bible tells us that Yahweh is love (see 1 John 4:8, 16b). He who does not love does not know Yahweh for Yahweh is love. Yahweh is love and anyone who abides in love abides in Yahweh and Yahweh in him.

Apostle Paul's letter to the Corinthians (chapter 13: 4-8) provides explanations of love; it says that love suffers long, love is kind, love does not puff itself, love does not envy, love does not parade, love does not behave rudely, love does not seek its own, and it is not provoked or thinks evil. Love does not rejoice in equity but rejoices in truth, bears all things, believes all things, hopes in all things, endures all things never fails. In support of this, 1 John 4:18 adds that: "There is no fear in love, but perfect love cast out fear because fear involves torment". Like all His attributes, Yahweh's love for humankind is immeasurable, is sacrificial, pure and is always unconditional. Yahweh wants us to revere Him in love and does not want us to fear Him as He does not torment us.

Yahweh revealed Himself to us as love as expressed in the Gospel of John (chapter 3:16): "For God so loved the world that He gave His only begotten Son, that whoever believes in Him should not perish, but have eternal life". Yeshua Ha Mashiach, the only begotten Son of Yahweh is given as a precious gift to all human-kind. That is unconditional love. Yahweh's love for us is unconditional. He demonstrated His own love for us in that, while we are still sinners, Christ died for us. John 15:13 expands more on the agape love of God, it says: "Greater love has no one than this, than to lay down one's life for a friend".

The love of Yahweh has been poured out into our hearts by the Holy Spirit who has been given to us (Romans 5:5). The love of Yahweh bears all the fruit of the Spirit as highlighted in Galatians 5:22-23. As children of God the scripture commands us to walk in love as Christ has loved us and has given himself to us, an offering to Yahweh for a sweet-smelling aroma" (Ephesians 5:1-2 NKJV). The least we can do for Yeshua Ha Mashiach is to walk in love as it is written in Mark 12: 30 - 31, "Love the

Lord your God with all your heart and with all your soul and with your entire mind and with all your strength. The second is this: Love your neighbor as yourself. There is no commandment greater than these". Love is the fundamental aspect of Yahweh and it covers most of the attributes that are in the introduction of the discussion of the nature of Yahweh as love.

YAHWEH IS HOLY

In my attempt to learn Hebrew, I learnt that the word for holy in Hebrew is "kodesh", it means: apartness, set-apartness, separateness, and/or sacredness. Taking from scriptures, I learnt that Yahweh's holiness denotes to His absolute ethical perfection and His indescribable Shekinah glory that is far above all He has created. The nature of Yahweh's holiness is well captured in many passages in the Bible. Some of which will be highlighted subsequently.

His holiness is demonstrated in His encounter with Moses out of the middle of the burning bush. The Bible tells us that when Yahweh called Moses and He issued this instruction: "Don't come close. Take off your scandals, for the place you are standing on is a holy ground" (Exodus 3:5). Further in Exodus 33 when Yahweh had face-to-face conversation with Moses at Mount Sinai, He appeared in His glory. We read that Moses said to Yahweh "Please show me Your glory" (18); Yahweh said, "I will make all my goodness to pass in front of you, and I will proclaim Yahweh's name before you, I will have mercy on which I will have mercy, and I will have compassion on whom I will have compassion (19). He said, you cannot see my face, for no one may see me and live" (20). Yahweh also said: "Behold, there is a place near me where you may stand on a rock (21). It will happen when my glory passes by, I will put you in a cleft in the rock and cover you with my hand until I have passed by (22), then I will take away my hand and you will see my back; but my face must not be seen" (23).

The effect of Yahweh's exhibition of His back to Moses was enough to cause the skin on his face to radiate with the glory of Yahweh. Aaron and the children of Israel were afraid to come near him (Exodus 34:30). Yahweh further declares His holiness in Lev. 20:7; He says, "Consecrate yourself therefore, and be holy for I am holy, Yahweh your Elohim".

The appearance of Yahweh to prophets Isaiah and Ezekiel as well as to John on the Island of Patmos is the testament of His indescribable holiness. The holiness of Yahweh pertaining His shekinah glory is well portrayed in Isaiah 6:1-4; Yahweh called Isaiah to be His prophet. Isaiah emphasised on how he saw Yahweh sitting on the throne, high and lifted up and the train of His robe filling up the temple. He continues to say that above the throne stood seraphim, each of which had six wings and with two hands he covered his face, and with two he covered his feet, and with two he flew. One cried to another and said holy, holy, holy is the Yahweh of hosts. The whole earth is full of His glory. And the posts of the door were shaken by the voice of him who cried out and the house was filled with smoke. That is the real shekinah glory.

Ezekiel chapter 1 relates his vision of Yahweh. Ezekiel also affirms the shekinah glory of Yahweh. Ezekiel 1 describes the shekinah glory of Yahweh, it says: "And above the firmament over their heads (the four living creatures) was the likeliness of a throne, in appearance like a sapphire stone, on the likeliness of a throne was a likeliness with the appearance of a man high above it (26). Also from the appearance of His waist and upwards, I saw as it were the colour of amber with the appearance of fire all around within it and from the appearance of His wait and downwards I saw, as it were the color of amber with the appearance of fire with brightness all around it (27) Like the appearance of a rainbow in a cloud on a rainy day so was the brightness all around it and verse 28 concludes thus: "that was the appearance of the glory of Yahweh".

In the last book of the Bible (Revelation) we read about John's vision when he was on the island of Patmos. John's vision is almost like Ezekiel's in that he saw the four living creatures and the throne. Isaiah and Ezekiel both saw Yahweh's throne and the four living creatures as seen by John were continuously proclaiming the holiness like the ones heard by Isaiah. In addition to the throne as seen by Isaiah and Ezekiel, John saw twenty-four thrones, twenty-four elders, and that from the throne proceeded lightning, thundering, and voices, seven lamps of fire which he calls the seven Spirits of Yahweh.

The four living creatures were also continuously proclaiming Yahweh's holiness, saying "Holy, holy, holy is Lord God the Almighty, Who was, and is and is to come" (Revelation 4:8). The Bible also tells us there are twenty four elders who were also worshipping Yahweh before the throne and sometimes in synchrony with the four living creatures. The twenty-four elders were proclaiming Yeshua Ha Mashiach's holiness; they said: "Worthy are You Our Lord and our God, the Holy One, to receive glory and honour and power. For You have created all things and because by Your desire they existed and were created" (Rev 4:11).

In synchrony they sang and glorified Him (Yeshua) before He opened the scroll and said: "You are worthy to take the scroll. And to open the seals for you were slain. And have redeemed us to Yahweh by Your blood. Out of every tribe and tongue and people and nations. And made us kings and priests to God. And we shall reign on the earth" (Revelation 5:9-10). The twenty-four elders' positions and actions during the worship tell us how they esteemed Yeshua's holiness. They fell down before Him and cast their crowns. That is real reverence.

The holiness of Yahweh does not only pertain to His glorious nature, but also that He is perfect in His ways. He is excellent in all He is. Yahweh is holy beyond our imagination. We need to worship Him for His splendor and beauty. We are called to be holy for He is Holy. Similar to His holiness is His righteousness which is discussed next.

Yahweh is righteous. What do I mean when I say Yahweh is righteous? The righteousness of Yahweh is one of His most prominent attributes. There is a thin line between His righteousness, His holiness and His goodness. On the other hand, His righteousness is closely associated with His justice. Simply put, it means Yahweh consistently acts according to His own character. He is consistent with His word. He is always true to His word. In Psalm 138:2 we read that He has magnified His word and His Name above all. In His righteousness He watches over His word to perform it as written in Jeremiah 1:12. He does not act contrary to His word. He is not measured by the standards of righteousness. He sets the standard of righteousness.

The entire Bible is full of Yahweh's righteousness. His righteousness is reflected in His word which encompasses His promises and in His actions. He always stands on His word. In Psalm 119 we read that Yahweh's word is forever settled in heaven. Referring to His righteousness, Yahweh says, "I Yahweh speak righteousness; I declare things that are right" (Isaiah 45:19b); Further in Isaiah 55 He says: "For as the rain comes down and as the snow from the sky, and does not return there, but waters the earth and makes it grow and bud, and gives seed to the sower and bread to the eater (10). So is the word that comes from my mouth, it will not return to me void, but will accomplish that which I please and will prosper in the thing I sent it to do" (11).

His righteousness as credited to His word is reflected in Ezra 9:15: "Yahweh, God of Israel You are righteous". Moses, the most recognised servant and prophet of Yahweh also acknowledged His righteousness as written in Deuteronomy 32:4: "The Rock, His work is perfect, for all His ways are just. A God of faithfulness who does no wrong, just and right is He". Throughout the Bible, Yahweh is continuously being praised for His righteousness. Some of the scriptures include but not limited to the following.

- Yahweh's words are flawless words, as silver is tried in a furnace on the earth, purified seven times (Psalm 12:6).
- Yahweh's precepts are right, rejoicing the heart. Yahweh's commandment is pure, enlightening the eyes (Psalm 19:8).
- Clouds and darkness surround Him. Righteousness and justice are the foundation of His throne (Psalm 97: 2).
- Your righteousness is an everlasting righteousness, and your law is truth (Psalm 119:142).
- Righteous are You, O! Yahweh, that I would plead my case with you; indeed, I would discuss matters of justice with you: Why has the way of the wicked prospered? Why are all those who deal in treachery at ease? (Jeremiah 12:1).
- You are righteous Yahweh. Your judgments are upright (Psalm 119:137).
- Your promises have been thoroughly tested, and Your servant loves them. (Psalm 119:140).

The purity of Yahweh's word is also emphasised by Samuel. We read in 2 Samuel 30:32 that Yahweh's words are pure and He is a shield to those who put their trust in Him. In 2 Samuel 22:31 it is written: "As for Yahweh, His way is perfect; Yahweh's word is tried. He is a buckler to all that trust Him".

As Yahweh's children, we have been made righteous with His righteousness. We are also called to live righteously, this is reflected in Hosea 10:12: "Sow for yourselves righteousness; reap according to kindness; break up your fallow ground, for it is time to seek Yahweh, until He comes and rains righteousness on you". We also encourage seeking first the kingdom of God and its righteousness. Seeking Yahweh's righteousness is accompanied by rewards".

Good examples of the rewards are given in Matthew 5: "Blessed are those who hunger and thirst for righteousness, for they shall be filled. Blessed are those who are persecuted for righteousness' sake, for theirs is the kingdom of heaven" (10). The word of God (Matthew 13:43) referring to the reward for the just on judgment day reads: "Then the righteous will shine forth as the sun in the kingdom of their Father. He who has ears to hear, let him hear"!

The next chapter focuses on Yeshua Ha Mashiach as Yahweh, "I AM THAT I AM". I hope this will enlighten the mind of your heart without causing any confusion. At this stage it suffices to say that Yahweh is Trinity although the word Trinity is not found in the Bible. Let me start by saying there is one God. According to 1 John 5:7, there are three that bear witness in heaven: the Father, the Word and the Holy Spirit and these three are one. The Trinity of God is three personal distinctions within the single divine essence. He is one in essence, personality and will. As individuals, they are called God and collectively they are still God.

SEVEN

YESHUA HA MASHIACH AS I AM THAT I AM

In the conclusion of the previous chapter I made mention of the Trinity of God. I also mentioned that God is one. The Father, the Son and the Holy Spirit are each God. Each is a distinct person. Important to note is that there is one God, who is the Father, one Lord, Yeshua Ha Mashiach and one Holy Spirit yet together they are one God. The individuality of God the Father and the Son is well expressed in 1 Corinthians 8:6: "Yet to us there is one God the Father, of whom we are, and we all things, and we for Him, and one Lord Yeshua Ha Mashiach, through Him all things are, and we live through Him".

Yeshua in John 10:30 stated that: "I and the Father are one". When Phillip, one of His disciples said to Him, Lord show us the Father (John 14:8), His response was: "Have I been with you for such a long time, and you do not know me Phillip? He who has seen me has seen the Father. How do you say show us the Father? (9). Do you not believe that I am in the Father and the Father is in me? The words that I tell you, I speak not from myself, but the Father who lives in me does His works (10). Believe me that I am in the Father, and the Father in me: or else believe me for the very works' sake" (11).

Significant to note is that there is perfect equality in dignity, nature, and honour between God the Father and Yeshua Ha Mashiach. What distinguishes the Father from the Son is the nature of subordination. Yeshua rightfully acknowledges that the Father is greater than Him. As the Son, He does what He sees the Father do and does the works of the Father who sent Him.

The power of meaning YHWH has been explained in the previous chapters. The name Yehoshua (shortened Yeshua) is contained in the Name Yahweh. Yeshua means Yahweh is my salvation. The Yod in the name Yeshua points to Him as the peg. Isaiah 22:23 reads, "I will fasten him as a glorious peg in a secure place. And he will become a glorious throne of his father's house. Yeshua is the right hand of power that reveals the nail that brings revelation. Yahweh is revealed in Yeshua. In John 14:7, 10 and 11. Yeshua said, "If you had known Me, you would have known the Father also, from now on you know Him and have seen Him (7). Do you not believe Me that I am in the Father and the Father in Me. The words that I speak to you, I do not speak on y authority, but the Father who dwells in e does the works (10). Believe that I am in the Father and the Father in Me, or else believe e for the sake of the works themselves" (11).

In chapter two I indicated that the letter H (Hey) represents revelation. The depth of the letter "H" also lies in that it is constituted by the first letter aleph א)) and the fourth letter dalet (ד (. The letter aleph represents a head in pictograph. The word dalet represents a door. A door is one of the of Yeshua. Most significantly, it stresses His humble nature. Yeshua humbled Himself to the point of death. I hope you still remember that the numerical value of hey is 5. One of the most significant meaning of the letter "h" is grace. It is by grace that we are saved.

The letter aleph (א) that is part of the letter hey (ה) points to Yeshua as the head of all that He created. Yeshua is the head of the body of Christ and all that He created. His supremacy is well reflected in Colossians 1:18. His headship is described in several scriptures (for example, 1 Corinthians 11:3. Ephesians 1: 22, Ephesians 5:23).

The letter H appears twice in the Name Yahweh. The repetition of the word "H" in the Name Yahweh emphasises that to Yeshua's revelation there is no end. Yeshua's name is contained in all the letters of YHWH. The word aleph (א) points to His oneness with Yahweh. They are indivisible.

Yeshua is our revelation. He is the one that is continually revealed to us. In the Bible, He is revealed from the book of Genesis to Revelation. Yeshua is the head of the revelation. Revelation is defined as the Spirit of the Messiah. Some of the as uttered by Yeshua stem from the word "H", For example, I am the door, I am the light of the world and I am the Alpha and Omega.

In Proverbs 29:18 we read that "Where there is no revelation, the people cast of restraint. But happy is the man who keeps the law". Yeshua said in John 15:7 that without Him we can do nothing. It is through His revelation of who He is, that we faith in Him. Revelation only comes by hearing the word.

One of the arguments of not using the Name Yahweh is that Yeshua never called the Name. In Genesis 1, the Bible tells us that Elohim, God in His plural form is the Creator. Taking into consideration that I AM that I AM refers to Yahweh, Yeshua identifies Himself in several scriptures as I AM. If we believe that Yeshua is the Word that was there in the beginning, the Word that was with Yahweh, the Word that became flesh, then we ought to understand that when he talked about Yahweh He said Father.

One would assume that as the Creator He knows the power of I AM. His declarations of I AM affirm that He is inseparable from Yahweh. John 14:11 reads: "I am in the Father and the Father is in Me". If you know Me then you know the Father, while John 10:30 reads: "I and My Father are one". He further asks us to believe that the Father is in Him and He is in the Father (John 10: 33b). In Hebrews 2:10b the scripture referring to Yeshua as the Creator reads: "For whom are all things and by whom are all things."

Yeshua Himself uttered several statements that confirm that He is the "I Am that I Am". Interestingly enough, the declared by Yeshua Ha Mashiach are mainly in the books of John and Revelation which are authored by one of His disciples, John. His first utterance of I Am is in the book of John 4:26 when He introduced Himself to the Samaritan woman and said I who speak am He, confirming that He is the Messiah who is known as Christ. Our Messiah came with a purpose of saving us from sin. He came that we may have life and that we may have it more abundantly (John 10:10b).

Below are the as spoken by Yeshua Ha Mashiach:

- I am the bread of life
- Before Abraham was I AM
- I am the door
- I am the good shepherd
- I am the resurrection and the life
- I am the way the truth and the life
- I am the vine
- I am the light of the world
- I am the one who bears witness of myself
- I am from above
- I am the Alpha and Omega

As we explore the Yeshua's I am's, let us bear in mind that they all meant to benefit us — His children. Take heed that His word that goes out of His mouth shall not return void but it shall accomplish what He pleases. It shall prosper in the thing for which He sent it (Isaiah 55:11). Each of the represents our spiritual needs from Him and they are prayer items in themselves. Let us look the following concise descriptions of the .

I AM THE BREAD OF LIFE

It is written "I am the bread of life, he who comes to Me will not hunger, and he who believes Me will never thirst (John 6:35). I am the bread of life (John 6:48). Verse 51 says, "I am the living bread which comes down from heaven. If anyone eats of this bread, he will live forever, and the bread that I shall give is My flesh, which I shall give for the life of the world". Yeshua is saying that He is all enough to all who come to Him.

Yeshua Ha Mashiach is essential in our lives, without Him we all experience spiritual starvation. He is our spiritual bread that gives eternal life. I liken Him to the shrew bread in the Holy Place in Exodus 25:30. So as the shrew bread that was in the tabernacle was taken and eaten, so we are called to eat the word on daily basis. Yeshua is the bread that comes from heaven and He is the word that was there in the beginning. We are commanded in the book of Joshua 1:8 not to let the book of law depart from our mouth but meditate on it day and night that we may observe to do according to all that is written in it; "For then you will make your way prosperous and you will have good success" (Joshua 1:8).

BEFORE ABRAHAM WAS, I AM (JOHN 8:58 NKJV)

In this scripture, He proclaimed His existence before Abraham; he said: "Most assuredly, I say to you before Abraham came into existence, I exist". This affirms that He is the image of the invisible God and the first born of all creation. In whom all things were created in heaven and on earth, visible or invisible, thrones of powers or rulers or authorities, all things were created through Him and for Him. He is before all things, and in all Him all things consist (Colossians 1:15-17). John 1:1 – 3 clearly states that Yeshua was both with Yahweh and was Yahweh, He was in the beginning with Yahweh and all things were made through Him, and without Him nothing was made. This includes Adam the first man, thus, before Abraham He is. Through the statement: before Abraham was I am, Yeshua was making it crystal clear that He is Yahweh, and that's what made the Jews try to kill Him.

I AM THE DOOR

I am the door, if anyone enters by Me, he will be saved, and will go in and out and find pasture (John 10:9). Yeshua is the entry point to our salvation. He is the door that ushers us to the Father for eternal life. There is no salvation in any other, for there is no other name under the heaven given among men by which we must be saved other than the name of Yeshua Ha Mashiach of Nazareth (Acts 4:12). He is able to save to the uttermost those who come to Yahweh through Him (Hebrews 7: 25a). Yeshua alone is the Saviour of the world. Anyone sneaking into a sheepfold by any means than the door is not there legitimately. Yeshua is that door and He alone offers the true path to salvation.

I AM THE GOOD SHEPHERD

Yeshua declared himself as a good shepherd in John 10:11 and 14. He declares Himself a good shepherd who gives His life for the sheep (John 10:11). He is a good shepherd that knows His sheep and that is also known by the sheep (John 10:14). The main roles of the shepherd as portrayed by Yeshua are: to look for and protect his own flock, to look for greener pastures and lead the sheep there. The good shepherd gives His life for the sheep (John 10:1).

The role of Yeshua as a good shepherd fulfills the word as written in Ezekiel 34: "For the Lord Yahweh says: Behold I Myself, even I will search for My sheep and will seek them out (11). As a shepherd seeks out his flock in the day among his sheep that are scattered abroad, so I will seek My sheep (12). I will feed them with good pasture, and their folds will be on the mountains of heights of Israel. There they will lie down in a good fold. They will feed on fat pasture on the mountains of Israel (14). I Myself will be the shepherd of my sheep and I will cause them to lie down, says the Lord Yahweh (15). I will seek that which was lost, and will bring back that which was driven away" (16a). This passage should be understood in the context that Yeshua and Abba Father are one as mentioned John 10:30: "I and My Father are one".

Further in Ezekiel 34:31, Yahweh referred to Himself as the shepherd of His people, He said: "You are my sheep, the sheep of My pasture, are men and I am your God, says the Lord Yahweh". What the Father is so is the Son thus Yeshua declares that He is a good Shepherd. Psalm 95 calls us to worship Him as His sheep, it says: "Oh! Come let us worship and bow down, let us kneel before our Maker (6). For He is our God. We are the people of His pasture, and the sheep of His care

(7). Today, oh that you would hear His voice (8)". In His declaration of Himself as a good shepherd, Yeshua stated that "My sheep hear my voice, I know them and they follow Me" (John 10:27).

Yeshua is the door and so much more. He is the Shepherd, the One whose voice the sheep know and trust. The shepherd will protect and save the sheep at any cost. Yeshua, as the Good Shepherd, died to save each of us. Greater love has He for us as His sheep. Romans 5:8 tells us that Yahweh demonstrates His own love towards us in that while we were sinners, Christ died for us.

I AM THE RESURRECTION AND THE LIFE

When Yeshua said: "I am the resurrection and the life" (John 11:25, 26), He was indicating that He is a source of both. There is neither resurrection nor life except through Him. Our Messiah is life; therefore, death has no ultimate power over Him. Romans 6:3-5 reads: "Or do you not know that as many as were baptised into Christ Yeshua, were baptised into His death, therefore we were buried with Him through baptism into death, that just as Christ was raised from the dead by the glory of Yahweh, even so we also should walk in newness of life. For if we have been united together in the likeliness of His death, certainly we also shall be in the likeliness of His resurrection" (NTL).

I AM THE WAY, THE TRUTH, AND THE LIFE

I am the way, the truth, and the life; No one comes to the Father except through me" (John 14:6). In these words Yeshua is declaring that He is the only path to eternity, the only true measure of righteousness and the source of life. Although Yeshua proclaimed Himself as the way, the truth and the life, for the purpose of this book, I will divide this statement into three parts and discuss each separately.

a. **I am the way.** In Acts 4:12 when Peter was talking about Yeshua Ha Mashiach of Nazareth He said: "Salvation is found in no one else, for there is no other name under heaven given to men by which we must be saved". The distinctive nature of Him as the only path to salvation is expressed in: I am the door; I am the way. In John 14:16c, Yeshua clearly states that no one comes to the Father except though Him. The way is reached through confession of Yeshua as the Lord. Romans 10 states that "If you confess with your mouth the; Lord Yeshua and believe in your heart, that Yahweh has raised Him from the dead you will be saved (9) For with the heart one believes unto righteousness and with the mouth confession is made unto salvation, For the scripture says whoever belies in Him will not be put to shame" (11).

b. **I am the truth.** The introduction in the book of John 1:1- 2 and 14 introduces Yeshua as the Word that was in the beginning, the Word that was with Yahweh, and the Word that was Yahweh and that the Word became flesh and dwelt among us and we beheld His glory, the glory of the father, full of grace and truth. The Word is truth. In John 17:17 when Yeshua was praying for His disciples, He said to Yahweh "Sanctify them by your truth. Your word is truth". The Bible is all about the truth of the word. Some of the scriptures that support this are provided below:

- Psalm 33:4: "For the word of Yahweh is right and all His work is done in truth".
- Psalm 119:160a declares that: "The entirety of your word is truth".
- Proverbs 30: "Every word of Yahweh is pure".

c. **I am the life:** Yeshua is the source of our lives. We are alive because He gives us the breath of life. Interestingly, as a life giver He also gives us the grace to live the life that He desires for us. We have the greatest manual that we need to follow — the word. If you believe that "All things were made through Him, and without Him nothing was made that was made, and in Him was life, and the life was the light of men (John 1:3-4, then you are enlightened to understand His claim that He is the life. Job acknowledges that life of every living thing and the breath of all mankind is in the hand of Yahweh (Job 12:10). Paul in Acts 17 while preaching in Athens, he proclaimed that God gives to all life and breath and all things (25).

Yeshua is the way to Abba Father, our way to our salvation. When we accept Him as our Lord and Saviour, He becomes the source of our truth. His word is living and active. He is the Word that was there in the beginning. When we come to Him, He gives us His Spirit who teaches us all we need to know. In Him we find the truth that set us free from any bondage and from the kingdom of darkness. In Him we live and have our being. As Life, He came that we may have life in abundance.

I AM THE TRUE VINE

Yeshua declares Himself as a true vine in John 15: 1, He says: "I am the true vine, and my Father is the vinedresser". He is the vine and we are the branches. A branch is highly dependent on the trunk for its nutrients and for production. A branch cannot bear fruits without the trunk. In essence the I am the vine is the source of our lives now and eternal. It is from Him as the vine that we have life in abundance. The fullness of Yeshua as the vine needs to be comprehended from all the benefits we have in Him through His crucifixion.

Interestingly, as the branches we are called to remain in Him and He promises to remain in us. He says, "Abide in Me and Me in you. As the branch cannot bear fruit on its own, neither can you, unless you abide in

Me" (John15:4). Yeshua is the source of our spiritual life; therefore, we need to stay connected. Further in verse 5 He emphasises that the branches cannot do anything without Him. He declares "I am the vine; you are the branches. He who abides in Me, and I in Him, bears much fruit for without me you can do nothing". As the source of life He is calling us to cling to Him.

I AM THE LIGHT OF THE WORLD (JOHN 8: 12B)

Yeshua revealed Himself as the light of the world to men who brought an adulterous woman to Him. He said to them "I am the light of the world. He who follows me shall not walk in darkness, but have the light of life". In John 9:5, He emphasised this by saying: "As long as I am in the world, I am the light of the world". Yeshua as the light of the world needs to be understood in the context that as Christians Yahweh has qualified us as partakers of the inheritance of the saints in the light and He has delivered us from the power of darkness and conveyed us into the kingdom of the Son of His love (Colossians 1: 12-13). Without light we are blind. No one is able to see without light; He is the light of the world. His word is light in our paths. While He was with His disciples in the world He was the light and He continues to be our light even today.

Yeshua referred to Himself as the light when He was predicting His death. He said to His disciples: "For a while longer the light is with you. Walk while you have light, lest darkness overtake you, he who walks in darkness does not know where he is going. While you have the light, believe in the light so that you may become sons of light" (John 12:35-36). Further in John 12:46 He says, "I have come as light into the world that whoever believes in me should not abide in darkness".

The prophecy about Yeshua as the light of the world was foretold in Isaiah (Isaiah 9:2 and 60:1-3), Isaiah prophesied thus: "The people who walked in darkness have seen great light. Those who dwell in the land of the shadow of death, upon them a light is shined". He further proclaimed: "Arise, shine. For your light has come. And the glory of the Yahweh is risen upon you. For behold darkness shall cover the earth. And deep darkness the people. But the Yahweh will arise over you. And His glory will be seen upon you. The Gentiles shall come to the light and the kings the brightness of your rising" (chapter 60:1-3). Light is equated to life. Before Yeshua introduced Himself as the light of the world in John 1: 4-5 and 9; He stated that in Him there was life, and life was the light of men. The light shines in darkness, and darkness did not comprehend it.

I AM THE ONE WHO BEARS WITNESS OF MYSELF

I am the one who bears witness of myself, for I know where I am going but you do not know where I come from and where I am going (John 8:14). This statement testifies to Him as omniscient, as the one who bears the wonderful counselor, Mighty God (Isaiah 9) and that He is the One that the Spirit of Yahweh is resting on. He is the Spirit of wisdom and understanding, the Spirit of counsel and might, the Spirit of knowledge of Yahweh, and the Spirit of fear of Yahweh. His ministry here on earth bears witness for Him as the Son of God. He alone does not need two or three witnesses of what He says. He is the true witness of Yahweh.

The certainty of Yeshua's witness is well captured in 1 John 5: "This is He who came by water and blood – Yeshua Ha Mashiach, not only by water, but by water and blood, and it is the Spirit who bears witness, because the Spirit is truth (6). For there are three that bear witness in heaven, namely, the Father, the word and the Holy Spirit and these three are one (7). And there are three that bear witness on earth: the Spirit, the water and the blood and these three agree as one".

In John 19:34, we read about how one of the soldiers pierced His side with a spear and immediately blood and water came out. The shepherd was to be smitten, the lamb was led to the slaughter, and therefore only by the shedding of His blood could Yeshua prove Himself to be the Messiah so long foretold. The blood that was shed on His crucifixion; Yeshua has made such expiation by His own blood, we know Him to be the Son of Yahweh. His blood is the seal of His mission, the very life of his work. The piercing of His side was prophecy fulfilled as written in John 10:36: "For these things took place that the Scripture might be fulfilled: 'Not one of his bones will be broken (Psalm 34:20). Zechariah 12:10 says, 'They will look on Him whom they have pierced'.

The Spirit of Yahweh that came upon Yeshua when He was baptised is the promised Holy Spirit that came upon His disciples on the Day of Pentecost. Yeshua declared that the Holy Spirit shall testify of Him. He said, "But when the Helper comes, whom I will send to you from the Father, the Spirit of truth who proceeds from the Father, He will testify of Me" (John 15:26).

I AM FROM ABOVE

I am from above and you are from this world (John 8:23). Yeshua confirmed His supremacy in (John 3:31) when He said, "He who comes from above is above all and he who comes from the earth is earthly and speaks of the earth". The scripture above as captured in the gospel of John the Baptist was declaring the supremacy of the Messiah. This is also supported by the Apostle Paul's letter to the church in Corinth (1 Cor.15:47); he says, "Adam, the first man was made from earth, while Yeshua; the second man came from heaven. Sin came through the first man while remission for sin came through the second man. He came with one purpose to save the world". The I am's declared by Yeshua as discussed above were spoken in the hearing of many. However, the in the book of Revelation are the words that He spoke to John in a vision while He was on the Island of Patmos. Next are the I am's depicted in the book of Revelation.

I AM THE ALPHA AND OMEGA, THE BEGINNING AND THE END (REV 1:8 11)

Let us look at the following scriptures that bear reference to this:

- I am He who lives and was dead and behold I am alive forevermore (Revelation 22:13).
- I am the Alpha and Omega, the Beginning and the End, the First and Last (Revelation 1:11 and 18)

Everything visible and invisible begins in Him. This is well captured in Colossians 1:15-17: "He is the image of the invisible God, the firstborn of all creation; because by means of him all [other] things were created in the heavens and upon the earth, the things visible and the things invisible, whether they are thrones or dominions, or principalities or powers. All things were created through Him and for Him. And He is before all things, and in Him all things consist". Everything, be it visible or invisible, has been created by Him. John 1:3 also tells us that all things were made through Him, and without Him nothing was made that was made. That makes Him Alpha, the beginning (Bereshith in Hebrew) of everything. In Hebrew, a word that is spoken three times denotes its intensity and seriousness.

Yeshua, as the Alpha and Omega, is the first and last in so many ways. He is the "author and finisher" of our faith (Hebrews 12:2), signifying that He begins it and carries it until it is finished. He is the fulfilling end of the Law (Matthew 5:17), and He is the beginning subject matter of the gospel of grace through faith, not of works (Ephesians 2:8-9). He is found in the first verse of Genesis and in the last verse of Revelation. He is the first and last, the all in all of salvation, from the justification before God to the final sanctification of His people.

Isaiah ascribes this aspect of Yeshua's essence as Alpha and Omega in several of His prophesies. For example:

- "I, the Lord, am the first, and with the last I am He" Isaiah (41:4).
- "I am the first, and I am the last; and besides Me there is no God" (Isaiah 44:6).
- "I am He; I am the first, I also am the last" (Isaiah 48:12).

This concurs with the prophecy that, "Of the increase of His government and peace there will be no end, upon the throne of David and over His Kingdom to order it and establish it with justice and judgment from that forward until forever". He is the first and last in a special way. He created us in our mother's wombs and we will spend eternity with Him. He is the door to Abba Father. No one can receive salvation except through Him. Lastly, we shall be with Him in the New Jerusalem. This description points to Him as the resurrected Yeshua Ha Mashiach who is the only begotten Son of Yahweh. The last "I AM" of Yeshua Ha Mashiach is in Revelation 16 (b) where He declares: "I am the Root and the Offspring of David, the Bright and the Morning Star". In this declaration, He is declaring His divine as well as His human nature.

Finally, brethren whatever things are true, whatever things are noble, and whatever things are just, whatever things are pure, whatever things are lovely, and whatever things are of good report. If there is anything of virtue, and if there is anything praiseworthy, meditate on these things (Philippians 4:8). I would say let your define the god you are; that is your I am that I am. As we respond to the call not to be conformed to the world, but to be transformed by the renewal of our minds, that we may prove what is the acceptable and perfect will of Yahweh (Romans:12:2), let our I am be aligned to the word of Yahweh. I believe that there is nothing wrong in calling Yahweh with all of His other titles such as Elohim, Adonai, Creator because these are His fitting titles. The main challenge is changing His real Name (Yahweh) to GOD, LORD and Jehovah in some Bibles.

Yahweh identified Himself with His personal Name for a reason. The Bible is full of scriptures that tell us to call upon His Name, proclaim His Name to all nations, pray in His Name, love His Name, praise His name, and bless His name. Yahweh is our Creator who delights in us (His creation) calling His Name; this is the assignment of this book — a call to restore His Name (Yahweh: יהוה).

As you call on the Name of Yahweh, let it be your free will. You have a choice to make. This book is intended to inform you that the God of the universe has a Name. His Name is Yahweh, יהוה. He has given you the right to call upon His Name. I hereby extend the invitation for you to join me to restore His Name Yahweh. Consider what is written in Deuteronomy 32 as you take a decision to call Him Yahweh or not. The scripture calls us to proclaim the Name of Yahweh; it says: "Give ear, O heavens, and I will speak, And hear, O earth, the words of my mouth. Let my teaching drop as rain. My speech distills as the dew, as raindrops on tender herb, and showers on grass. For I proclaim the name of Yahweh. Ascribe greatness to our Elohim".

In conclusion, I personally find the use of the divine Name of Yahweh quite powerful and moving. I called upon the Name of Yahweh and He upheld me. I am the least but He assigned me to restore His Name, Yahweh. Once more you have a choice. I however, respect the tradition that seeks to protect Yahweh's Name from abuse. My last appeal is that, keep your Bible however, wherever you find the word GOD, LORD or Jehovah rather read it as Yahweh.

The name Yahweh is a map to our spiritual journey. It is a navigator to our salvation. It is the revelation of our grace. Contained in the Name Yahweh is the first and foremost truth about God: He exists, He is all powerful, all knowing, He is eternal. Yahweh is the only God.

ANNEXURE

THE TITLES OF YAHWEH.

His name is Yahweh: The self-existing One (Genesis 2:4)
Elohim-God: The strong Creator (Genesis 1:1)
Adonai-Lord/Master: The headship name (Genesis 15:2)

**THE COMPOUND TITLES YAHWEH EL AND
YAHWEH ELOHIM: THE LORD GOD**

Yahweh El Elohim: The Lord God of gods (Joshua 22:22)
Yahweh Elohim: The Lord God (Genesis 2:4, 3:9-13, 21)
Yahweh Elohe Abothekem: The Lord God of your Fathers (Joshua 18:3)
Yahweh El Elyon: The Lord, the Most High God (Genesis 14:22)
Yahweh El Emeth: Lord God of truth (Psalms 31:5)
Yahweh El Gemuw al: The Lord God of recompenses (Jeremiah 51:56)
Yahweh Elohim Tsebaoth: Lord God of hosts (Psalm 59:5, Isaiah 28:22)
Yahweh Elohe Yeshuati: Lord God of my salvation (Psalm 88:1)
Yahweh Elohe Yisrael: The Lord God of Israel (Psalm 41:13)

THE COMPOUND NAMES:
EL, ELOHIM, AND ELOHE: GOD

Elohim: God (Genesis 1:1)

Elohim Bashamayim: God in Heaven (Joshua 2:11)

El Bethel: God of the House of God (Genesis 35:7)

Elohe Chaseddi: The God of my mercy (Psalms 59:10)

Elohe Yisrael: God, the God of Israel (Genesis 33:20)

El Elyon: The Most High God (Genesis 14:18, Daniel 3:26, Psalms 78:56)

El Emunah: The faithful God (Deuteronomy 7:9)

El Gibbor: Mighty God (Isaiah 9:6)

El Hakabodh: The God of glory (Psalms 29:3)

El Hay: The living God (Joshua 3:10, Jeremiah 23:36, Daniel 3:26)

El Hayyay: God of my life (Psalms 42:8)

Elohim Kedoshim: Holy God (Joshua 24:19)

El Kanna: Jealous God (Exodus 20:5, Joshua 24:19)

Elohe Mauzi: God of my strength (Psalms 43:2)

Elohim Machase Lanu: God our refuge (Psalms 62:8)

Eli Maelekhi: God my king (Psalms 68:24)

El Marom: God Most High (Micah 6:6)

El Nekamoth: God who avengeth (Psalms 18:47)

El Nose: God that forgave (Psalms 99:8)

Elohenu Olam: Our everlasting God (Psalms 48:14)

Elohim Ozer Li: God my helper (Psalms 54:4)

El Rai: God sees me (Genesis 16:13)

El Sali: God, my rock (Psalms 42:9)

El Shaddai: Almighty God (Genesis 17:1, 2; Ezekiel 10:5)

Elohim Shoptim Ba-arets: God who judges in the earth (Psalm 58:1)

El Simchath Gili: God my exceeding joy (Psalms 43:4)

Elohim Tsebaoth: God of hosts (Psalms 80:7, Jeremiah 35:17 & 38:17)

Elohe Tishuathi: God of my salvation (Psalms 18:46 & 51:14)

Elohe Tsadeki: God of my righteousness (Psalms 4:1)

Elohe Yakob: God of Israel (Psalms 20:1)

Elohe Yisrael: God of Israel (Psalms 59:5)

The Compound Titles Yahweh: The Lord (Exodus 6: 2 & 3)

Adonai Yahweh: Lord God (Genesis 15:2)

Yahweh Adon Kol Ha-arets: The Lord, the Lord of all the earth (Joshua 3:11)

Yahweh Bore: The Lord Creator (Isaiah 40:28)

Yahweh Chereb: The Lord the sword (Deuteronomy 33:29)

Yahweh Eli: The Lord my God (Psalms 18:2)

Yahweh Elyon: The Lord Most High (Genesis 14:18-20)

Yahweh Gibbor Milchamah: The Lord mighty in battle (Psalms 24:8)

Yahweh Maginnenu: The Lord our defense (Psalms 89:18)

Yahweh Goelekh: The Lord thy redeemer (Isaiah 49:26 & 60:16)

Yahweh Hashopet: The Lord the judge (Judges 11:27)

Yahweh Hoshiah: O Lord save (Psalms 20:9)

Yahweh Immeka: The Lord Is with you (Judges 6:12)

Yahweh Izuz Wegibbor: The Lord strong and mighty (Psalms 24:8)

Yahweh –Jireh: The Lord shall provide (Genesis 22:14)

Yahweh Kabodhi: The Lord my God (Psalms 3:3)

Yahweh Kanna Shemo: The Lord whose name is jealous (Exodus 34:14)

Yahweh Keren Yishi: The Lord the horn of my salvation (Psalm 18:2)

Yahweh Machsi: The Lord my refuge (Psalm 91:9)

Yahweh Magen: The Lord the shield (Deuteronomy 33:29)

Yahweh Makkeh: The Lord who strikes (Ezekiel 7:9)

Yahweh Mauzzam: The Lord their strength (Psalms 37:39)

Yahweh Mauzzi: The Lord my fortress (Jeremiah 16:19)

Ha-Melech Yahweh: The Lord the king (Psalms 98:6)

Yahweh Melech Olam: The Lord king forever (Psalms 10:16)

Yahweh Mephalti: The Lord my deliverer (Psalms 18:2)

Yahweh Mekaddishkem: The Lord that sanctifies you (Exodus 31:13)

Yahweh Metsudhathi: The Lord my high tower (Psalms 18:2)

Yahweh Moshiekh: The Lord your saviour (Isaiah 49:26 & 60:16)

Yahweh Nissi: The Lord my banner (Exodus 17:15)

Yahweh Ori: The Lord my light (Psalms 27:1)

Yahweh Uzzi: The Lord my strength (Psalms 28:7)

Yahweh Rophe: The Lord (our) healer (Exodus 15:26)

Yahweh Rohi: The Lord My shepherd (Psalms 23:1)

Yahweh Sabaoth (Tsebaoth): Lord the of hosts (I Samuel 1:3)

Yahweh Sali: The Lord my rock (Psalms 18:2)

Yahweh Shalom: The Lord (our) peace (Judges 6:24)

Yahweh Shammah: The Lord is there (Ezekiel 48:35)

Yahweh Tsidkenu: The Lord our righteousness (Jeremiah 23:6)

Yahweh Tsuri: O Lord my strength (Psalms 19:14)

References

Cohen O and Baker S: 2012. Biblical Hebrew B: eTeachergroup: Israel

http;// atrumputinthe wilderness.org/secretsofthename. thm

http://encyclopedia.com/religion/enclopedias-almanacs-transcripts and maps/ god names. Viewed on 12 February 2018

http:/www.hebrew4chistians.com/ Grammar / Unit/Unit One/ Aleph-Bet/Yod/yod.htmlttps//www.beth-tsedec.org. Accessed 20 January 2018

http://hebrew4christians .com. Names of G-g.yhwh/yhth .html

http:/shekinah.elysimgates.com / Hebrew.htm. Viewed 16 June 2017

Kubik G. The Sacred Name: YWHH.. Homepagegregorykubik, Accessed 15 November 2017

Kohi, F. (2015). Names of God in Christianity; en.wikipedia.org//wiki// Name of God_in _Christianity: Accessed on 28 November 2018.

Lilly of the valley: The names of God. www. Lilly of the Valley: Virginia. Viewed 15 August 2017

Pipe, J. (1984). Devotional I am who I am. https://www.desiringgod.org/messages/i-am-who-i-am

Rebjeff.com//blog/vaeira-god

Spangler, A. (2012). Praying the names of God: Zondervan: China

Snyder, N. (2011). His Name is Yahweh. Townville: United States

The Kings University. (2015). Holy Scriptures Tree of Life Version. Baker Books: Michigan

The Bible: Hebrew– English:2008: Sinai Publishing: Israel

The Holy Bible: New King James Version.1996. Broadman and Holman: Korea

Yahweh's Word: The Holy Bible: 2017

www.ingramcontent.com/pod-product-compliance
Lightning Source LLC
Chambersburg PA
CBHW050007070726
47592CB00018B/1076